CHILTERN
WALKS

OXFORD
&
WEST BUCKINGHAMSHIRE

Nick Moon

This book is one of a series of three to provide a comprehensive coverage of walks throughout the whole of the Chiltern area (as defined by the Chiltern Society). The walks included vary in length from 3.0 to 10.9 miles, but are mainly in the 5- to 7-mile range popular for half-day walks, although suggestions of possible combinations of walks are given for those preferring a full day's walk.

Each walk gives details of nearby places of interest and is accompanied by a specially drawn map of the route which also indicates local pubs and a skeleton road network.

The author, Nick Moon, has lived in or regularly visited the Chilterns all his life and has, for over 25 years, been an active member of the Chiltern Society's Rights of Way Group, which seeks to protect and improve the area's footpath and bridleway network. Thanks to the help and encouragement of the late Don Gresswell MBE, he was introduced to the writing books of walks and has since written or contributed to a number of publications in this field.

OTHER PUBLICATIONS BY NICK MOON

Chiltern Walks Trilogy
Chiltern Walks 1 :   Hertfordshire, Bedfordshire and
                        North Buckinghamshire :
                        Book Castle new edition 2001
Chiltern Walks 2 :   Buckinghamshire : Book Castle new edition 1997
Chiltern Walks 3 :   Oxfordshire and West Buckinghamshire :
                        Book Castle new edition 2001

Oxfordshire Walks
Oxfordshire Walks 1 :   Oxford, The Cotswolds and
                        The Cherwell Valley : new edition 1998
Oxfordshire Walks 2 :   Oxford, The Downs and the
                        Thames Valley : new edition 2001

Family Walks
Family Walks 1: Chilterns – South : 1997
Family Walks 2: Chilterns – North : 1998

The D'Arcy Dalton Way across the Oxfordshire Cotswolds
and Thames Valley : 1999

The Chiltern Way : 2000

First published May 1992
New edition June 1996
New edition July 2001
by The Book Castle
12 Church Street, Dunstable, Bedfordshire

Computer Typeset by J. L. Miller, Aldbury, Herts
Printed in Great Britain by Antony Rowe Ltd., Chippenham, Wilts.

ISBN 1 871199 36 0

Contents

POSSIBLE LONGER WALKS PRODUCED BY COMBINING WALKS DESCRIBED IN THE BOOK

Walks	Miles	Km
2 + 3	11.6	18.6
2 + 3 + 4	17.0	27.3
2 + 3 + 4 + 5B	21.7	34.9
2 + 3 + 4 + 6B	19.9 or 20.2	32.1 or 32.6
3 + 4	11.1	17.9
3 + 4 + 5A	22.0	35.4
3 + 4 + 5B	15.8	25.5
3 + 4 + 6A	15.5 or 15.8	25.0 or 25.5
3 + 4 + 6B	14.1 or 14.4	22.7 or 23.2
4 + 5A	16.3	26.2
4 + 5B	10.1	16.3
4 + 6A	9.8 or 10.1	15.8 or 16.3
4 + 6A + 28	15.2 or 15.5	24.5 or 25.0
4 + 6B	8.4 or 8.7	13.5 or 14.0
4 + 6B + 28	14.3	23.0
6A + 28	11.4 or 11.7	18.4 or 18.9
6A + 28 + 27	17.5	28.2
6B + 28	9.6 or 9.9	15.5 or 16.0
6B+ 28 + 27	15.7	25.3
7 + 22	12.0	19.4
8 + 11A	15.3	24.6
8 + 11 (A – B)	12.3	19.7
18 + 19	12.2	19.6
23 + 24	12.3 or 12.9	19.8 or 20.8
23 + 25	16.4	26.4
24 + 25	16.8 or 17.2	27.1 or 27.7
27 + 28	11.3 or 11.6	18.2 or 18.8

Cover Photograph: © Nick Moon. Approaching Turville in Autumn (Walk 28)

Introduction

This book of walks is one of three to cover the whole of the Chilterns
from the Goring Gap on the River Thames to the Hitchin Gap in North
Hertfordshire. The area covered by this volume includes the whole of
the Oxfordshire Chilterns as well as the adjoining part of the
Buckinghamshire Chilterns west of a line from Princes Risborough to
Marlow and as such contains what many people believe to be some of
the best Chiltern scenery. Be that as it may, within this area are to be
found a wealth of varied landscapes, all of which have much to offer
the walker. On the north-western edge, there is the escarpment, parts
of which are very steep, where woodland is interspersed with
spectacular downland with at its foot a whole string of historic villages
situated near springs which, in the past, saved their inhabitants from
the water supply problems experienced in the hills. To the west and
south, the area is bounded by what must, without doubt, be the most
beautiful section of the Thames Valley from Wallingford through the
narrow steep-sided Goring Gap and winding its way through the hills
to Marlow. This part of the valley can be sub-divided into several
distinct sections, each of which has its own particular attractions to
the walker. Between Wallingford and Goring, the river runs at the
foot of a shallower section of the escarpment than further north with
rolling largely treeless foothills offering panoramic views across the
valley and along the line of the Berkshire Downs to the west. From
Goring to Reading the scene changes completely to a deep valley
encased between wooded hills, while from Reading to Shiplake the
mainly agricultural dip slope of the Chilterns rises gently from the
valley offering a combination of panoramic views and easy walking.
Beyond Shiplake, however, the river resumes its passage through a
deep valley between steep wooded hills providing an idyllic setting for
both walking and boating. Within the U-shaped area created by these
natural boundaries, the countryside south of the A4130 is a
heavily-wooded upland plateau traversed by shallow bottoms dropping
gently from the low escarpment on the west side of the river bend to
the east side of the bend and if scenically less spectacular than other
areas, provides quiet easy walking beautified by copious woodland.
North of the A4130, however, lies the unspoilt heart of the Chilterns
with picturesque deep valleys such as Bix Bottom and the Stonor,
Hambleden, Turville and Wormsley valleys interspersed by ranges of
wooded hills which thankfully escaped pre-war ribbon development
and have since been preserved by the town and country planning

5

system. Finally, north-east of the B482, lies the western part of the Wycombe country, which, although it has suffered more from development than much of the rest of the area covered by this book, remains fine walking country thanks to its steep-sided ridges and bottoms and a generous scattering of beechwoods.

The majority of walks included in this book are in the 5 – 7 mile range, which is justifiably popular for half-day walks, but, for the less energetic or for short winter afternoons, a few shorter versions are indicated in the text, while others can be devised with the assistance of a map. In addition, a number of walks in the 7 – 11 mile range are included for those preferring a leisurely day's walk or for longer spring and summer afternoons, while a list of possible combinations of walks is provided for those favouring a full day's walk of up to 22 miles.

Details of how to reach the starting points by car and where to park are given with each walk and any convenient railway stations are shown on the accompanying plan. Information on bus routes and operators can be obtained by telephoning 0870 608 2608.

All the walks described here follow public rights of way, use permissive paths across land owned by public bodies or cross public open space. As the majority of walks cross land used for economic purposes such as agriculture, forestry or the rearing of game, walkers are urged to follow the Country Code at all times:
- Guard against all risk of fire
- Fasten all gates
- Keep dogs under proper control
- Keep to the paths across farmland
- Avoid damaging fences, hedges and walls
- Leave no litter – take it home
- Safeguard water supplies
- Protect wild life, wild plants and trees
- Go carefully on country roads on the right-hand side facing oncoming traffic
- Respect the life of the countryside

Observing these rules helps prevent financial loss to landowners and damage to the environment, as well as the all-too-frequent and sometimes justified bad feeling towards walkers in the countryside.

While it is hoped that the special maps provided with each walk will assist the user to complete the walks without going astray and skeleton details of the surrounding road network are given to enable walkers to shorten the routes in emergency, it is always advisable to take an Ordnance Survey or Chiltern Society map with you to enable you to shorten or otherwise vary the routes without using roads or get your bearings if you do become seriously lost. Details of the appropriate maps are given in the introductory information of each walk.

As for other equipment, readers are advised that some mud will normally be encountered on most walks particularly in woodland except in the driest weather. However proper walking boots are to be recommended at all times, as, even when there are no mud problems, hard ruts or rough surfaces make the protection given by boots to the ankles desirable. In addition, the nature of the countryside makes many Chiltern paths prone to overgrowth, particularly in summer. To avoid resultant discomfort to walkers, protective clothing is advisable, especially where specific warnings are given.

Some of the walks may be familiar to readers as they were previously published in the 'Walks for Motorists : Chilterns (Southern Area)' which is now out of print, but about half are completely new or have been radically altered, while all of the old walks have been rechecked and brought up to date. In addition, as the walks are now appearing in the Chiltern Society's name, all the path numbers have been shown on the plans and incorporated into the texts. These numbers, which are also shown on the Society's Footpath Maps, consist of the official County Council footpath number with the prefix letters used by the Society to indicate the parish concerned. It is therefore most helpful to use these when reporting any path problems you may find, together, if possible, with the national grid reference for the precise location of the trouble spot, as, in this way, the problem can be identified on the ground with a minimum of loss of time in looking for it. National grid references can, however, only be calculated with the help of Ordnance Survey Landranger, Explorer or Pathfinder maps and an explanation of how this is done can be found in the Key to all Landranger and Explorer maps.

The length of time required for any particular walk depends on a number of factors such as your personal walking speed, the number of hills, stiles etc. to be negotiated, whether or not you stop to rest, eat or drink, investigate places of interest etc. and the number of impediments such as mud, crops, overgrowth, ploughing etc. which you encounter, but generally an average speed of between two and two and a half miles per hour is about right in the Chilterns. It is, however, always advisable to allow extra time if you are limited by the daylight or catching a particular bus or train home in order to avoid your walk developing into a race against the clock.

Should you have problems with any of the paths used on the walks or find that the description given is no longer correct, the author would be most grateful if you could let him have details (c/o The Book Castle), so that attempts can be made to rectify the problem or the text can be corrected at the next reprint. Nevertheless, the author hopes that you will not encounter any serious problems and have pleasure from following the walks.

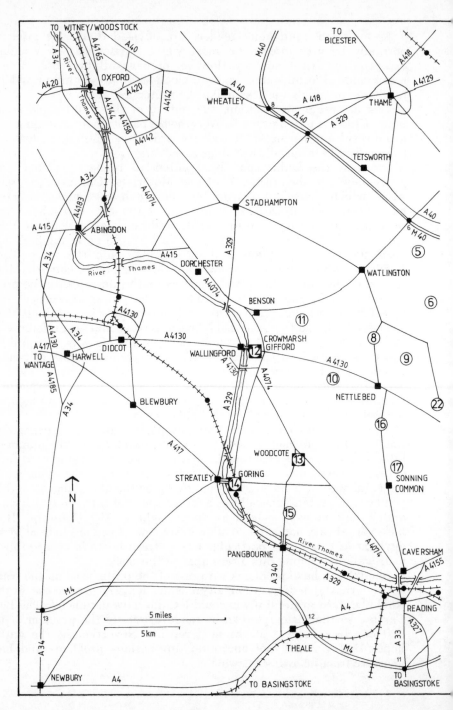

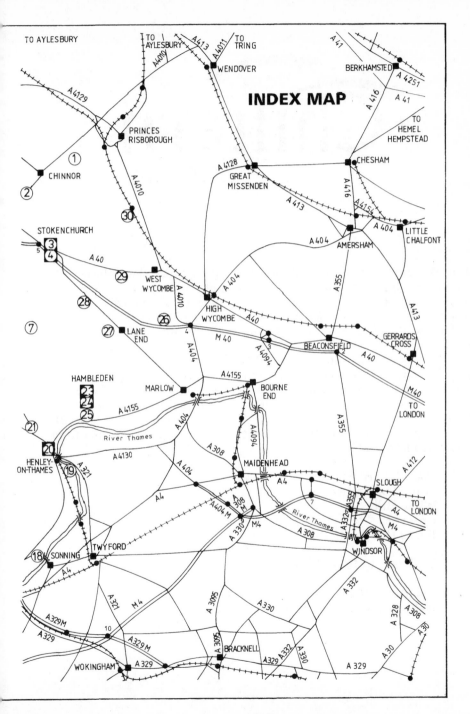

INDEX MAP

The Chiltern Society was founded in 1965 with the objects: 'To encourage high standards of town and country planning and architecture and to stimulate public interest in and care for the beauty, history and character of the area of the Chiltern Hills.'

The Society Rights of Way Group actively protects and restores public rights of way in the Chilterns – some 5,000 paths. It has surveyed every individual path and takes up irregularities with local parish councils, district or county councils to preserve public rights. It organises voluntary working parties most weekends to clear, waymark or otherwise encourage the use of paths for the public to enjoy the Chiltern countryside. Details of the Society's activities and footpath maps as well as membership application forms can be obtained from the Administrator:

> The Chiltern Society
> White Hill Centre
> White Hill
> Chesham
> Bucks HP5 1AG
>
> Tel/Fax: 01494–771250
>
> e.mail :   chiltern.society@cwcom.net
> Web site : www.chilternsociety.freeserve.co.uk

WALK 1: Bledlow

Length of Walk: 5.3 miles / 8.5 Km

Starting Point: Telephone box in Church End, Bledlow.

Grid Ref: SP777021

Maps: OS Landranger Sheet 165
OS Explorer Sheet 181 (or old Sheet 2)
OS Pathfinder Sheets 1117 (SP60/70) & 1118 (SP80/90)
Chiltern Society FP Map No.7.

How to get there / Parking: Bledlow, 2 miles southwest of Princes Risborough, may be reached from the southern end of the town by taking the B4444 towards Longwick to reach the B4009. Turn left onto this and after 1 mile, turn left into Perry Lane, signposted to 'Bledlow Ridge/Wycombe'. Follow it for half a mile, then turn right into Church End. After passing the church, continue for a further 150 yards to a parking area on the right on either side of the village telephone box.

Bledlow village, on the lower slopes of Wain Hill where the Risborough gap in the Chiltern hills meets the Vale of Aylesbury, is now a picturesque Chiltern backwater, but it has an obviously strategic location and a history to match. Evidence of settlement in the Bronze Age has been found in nearby woods, but references to the village itself go back at least a thousand years. Its name, recorded in 1012 as 'Bleddanhlaew', though undoubtedly of Anglo-Saxon origin, is variously said to mean 'Bledda's Hill' or 'Bloody Hill', the latter interpretation being thought to refer to a battle near the village between the Saxons and the Vikings. In 1066, it is thought to have been visited and sacked by William the Conqueror's army. The village today can boast a largely unaltered thirteenth-century church with a carved Norman font, fourteenth-century murals and heraldic glass and nearby are some attractive sixteenth-century timbered cottages with herring-bone brickwork and the early eighteenth-century manor house which, since 1801, has been the property of the Carrington family.

WALK 1

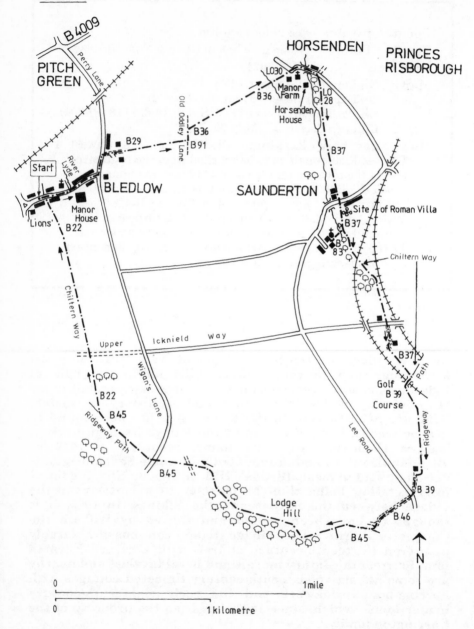

The walk, which is of a generally easy nature, first takes you across the Risborough gap to the fascinating 'lost villages' of Horsenden and Saunderton and then circles by way of the Chiltern Way and Ridgeway Path to Lodge Hill, where neolithic tools and bronze age burial mounds and pottery have been found, before returning to Bledlow.

Starting from the telephone box in Church End, Bledlow, walk north-eastwards along the road passing the church, the manor house and the Lyde Garden. On reaching a T-junction, turn left into Perry Lane and after some 150 yards, just before the first right-hand cottage, turn right into a rough lane (path B29). Where the lane forks, take the left-hand option straight on, crossing a stile by a gate and following a macadam drive straight on through gates to a gate and stile into a field. Cross the stile and follow a right-hand hedge straight on through two fields with Whiteleaf Cross coming into view on the hillside ahead. At the far end of the second field, cross a stile into byway B91, an old green lane called Old Oddley Lane and turn left along it. After about 70 yards, turn right through a hedge gap and take path B36, following a left-hand hedge. At the far end of this field, take what is normally a crop break straight on across the next field to a culvert and stile. Cross these and take path LO30 straight on to the corner of a hedge, then follow the hedge straight on to reach a bend in Horsenden village street by the church, a pond and Manor Farm.

Horsenden must once have been a much larger village than it is today. Formerly an independent parish, its fifteenth-century church was reduced in size in 1765 when its ruinous nave was demolished and the present tower was constructed in its place at the end of the chancel. This is the reason for its unusual appearance and it suggests that the depopulation of the village had already taken place by this date.

Now follow the village street straight on for some 200 yards, passing the church and Horsenden House to your right and some picturesque cottages to your left. Just past a thatched cottage called Gate Cottage, turn right over a stile by a white gate onto path LO28 and follow it (later path B37) beside a right-hand belt of trees concealing a brook and a series of lakes through three fields to reach a kissing-gate. Go through this and follow a left-hand fence through a garden passing a cottage. By a garage, join a macadam drive and follow it straight on to reach a road at Saunderton.

Cross this road and take path B37 between hedges straight on to a rail-stile leading into a field at the site of a Roman villa, then follow the right-hand hedge straight on. If wishing to visit Saunderton's restored thirteenth-century church with its original font, an ancient brass and mediaeval tiles, where the hedge bears left, turn right through a gap in the hedge onto path B83, part of the Chiltern Way, which leads you through marshland flanking a brook and soon emerges through a kissing-gate into the churchyard. Otherwise take path B37 joining the Chiltern Way and following the right-hand hedge straight on through two fields to a kissing-gate and flight of steps leading to a railway line. Cross this carefully and continue through a further kissing-gate into a field. Now follow a right-hand hedge straight on and, where the hedge ends, continue straight on across a field, walking parallel to the fence of another railway to your left, to reach the near left-hand corner of a hedge surrounding a white house. Now follow this hedge straight on to a hedge gap onto the Upper Icknield Way. Having crossed this ancient road, take the macadam drive of the Old Rectory (still path B37) straight on passing the eighteenth-century house and crossing a stile in the rear right-hand corner of the garden. Now go straight on to reach a kissing-gate on the Ridgeway Path (B39). Leaving the Chitern Way and joining the Ridgeway Path, go through this and continue through scrub to recross the railway, then cross a stile which leads to a golf course. Now follow a fenced path across the golf course for nearly 300 yards, soon turning left and eventually reaching a stile leading off the course. Cross this and go straight on across a field, heading just left of a house to reach the corner of its fence. Follow this fence straight on, then, where it turns right, follow it to join a gravel drive, continuing along this to reach Lee Road. Cross this road and go through a hedge gap opposite onto bridleway B46, a grassy track following a left-hand hedge. Soon after the hedge bears left, in a corner of the field turn right and take bridleway B45 following a left-hand hedge gently climbing with superb views to right and left. On reaching a thick hedge, go straight on through it and follow a left-hand hedge uphill. Disregard a crossing track and now on footpath B45, where the hedge ends, go straight on uphill. Having passed a broken-down fence to your right, bear half right following an obvious path along the downland ridge of Lodge Hill with panoramic views of the Risborough gap and Vale of Aylesbury beyond.

At the far end of the ridge, continue straight on downhill through scrub eventually emerging into the corner of a field. Now follow the left-hand hedge straight on to a kissing-gate in it. Here turn left and follow what is normally a crop break straight across a field, ignoring a crossing bridleway and heading for a kissing-gate just right of an orange-capped white post marking an underground gas pipeline. Go through this kissing-gate and bear half left to a kissing-gate in a corner of the field leading to Wigan's Lane. Bear half left across this road to go through a kissing-gate virtually opposite, then take path

B45 following a left-hand hedge straight on. After about 300 yards ignore a stile in the hedge leading into a field corner, then, rejoining the Chiltern Way, a little further on, transfer through a kissing-gate to the other side of the hedge and continue straight on for a further 100 yards to a stile in the right-hand fence. Turn right over this and a second stile onto path B22, here leaving the Ridgeway Path and bear half left downhill to cross a stile into a fenced plantation. Now go straight on uphill through the plantation to cross another stile, then continue ahead over a rise to a stile leading to the Upper Icknield Way. Cross this ancient green lane and another stile then follow a right-hand hedge straight on through two fields to a stile leading to a path between gardens at Bledlow which brings you out to the village street near your starting point.

WALK 2:   Crowell

Length of Walk: 6.1 miles / 9.9 Km

Starting Point: Crowell village green.

Grid Ref: SU744997

Maps: OS Landranger Sheet 165
OS Explorer Sheets 171 & 181 (or old Sheets 2 & 3)
OS Pathfinder Sheets 1117 (SP60/70) & 1137 (SU69/79)
Chiltern Society FP Map No. 14

How to get there / Parking: Crowell, 4.5 miles southeast of
Thame, may be reached by leaving the M40 at Junction 6
(Lewknor) and following the B4009 towards Chinnor for
just over 2 miles, turning right onto the village green just
past a sign to Crowell Church. Very limited parking space
exists here, but extra space is available on rough lanes
leading off the B4009 towards or away from the
escarpment.

Crowell, a small village below the escarpment sandwiched
between two larger neighbours, Chinnor and Kingston Blount,
has, hitherto, managed to preserve its identity and its status
as an independent parish against all apparent odds. The
parish, the name of which is thought to mean 'Crow's well', is
typical for those along the foot of the Chiltern escarpment or
the Thames, in being a long strip over 3 miles long, but only
half a mile wide and bears the curious distinction of being the
last parish in Oxfordshire (and possible the whole country) to
be inclosed, its award only having been made in 1882. This is,
however, not its only claim to fame, as the 'Shepherd's Crook',
which may have had to be rebuilt in 1859 when a large fire
destroyed much of the village, is alleged to have had John
Bunyan as a guest, while the sixteenth-century farmhouse,
Ellwood House, on the other side of the B4009 was, in 1639, the
birthplace of Thomas Ellwood, a prominent Quaker and a
friend of John Milton. It was he who rented the cottage at
Chalfont St. Giles to enable Milton to escape the Great Plague
in 1665 and inspired the poet to write 'Paradise Regained'. The
village's oldest building, however, is the Norman church,
largely rebuilt in 1878, but preserving some of the original
twelfth-century building.

The walk, which follows ancient and largely disused roadways for much of its length, takes in escarpment beechwoods, the picturesque village of Aston Rowant and some extensive views of the escarpment from below.

Starting from Crowell village green in front of the 'Shepherd's Crook', take CR17, the lane out of the back left-hand corner of the village green, towards the escarpment. Soon the village and the macadam surface are left behind and after a quarter mile, a hump in the stony road marks a former level crossing on the Watlington Branch Line (opened in 1872 and closed in 1957). Just beyond this to the left is the vast chalk quarry of the former Chinnor Cement Works. Go straight on and at the far side of the quarry, cross the Upper Icknield Way, an ancient Celtic road named after Boadicea's people, the Iceni. Despite being more dangerous in the past, because of robbers, than the Lower Icknield Way, the upper road was preferred in wet weather as a drier route.

Continue straight on up a hedged lane (CR6), the ancient road from Crowell to High Wycombe. On entering Crowell Hill Wood, go straight on along a track in the bottom of a deep gully, which climbs steadily and widens out near the top of the hill before emerging onto the bend of a road at Crowell Hill. On reaching the road, follow it straight on for about 60 yards and then turn right onto a waymarked path (CR8) inside the edge of the wood. Follow this path for a third of a mile, ignoring all tracks going deeper into the wood. This part of the woodland, which is 800 feet above sea-level, is known by the self-explanatory name Gypsies' Plain. Where the edge of the wood turns sharply away to the left, go straight on along the waymarked path. After a further 150 yards, the waymarked path crosses a raised track, bears half left and (now as AR23) shortly becomes flanked by a boundary ridge to the left and coniferous woodland to the right.

After a quarter mile, a sunken track in the bottom of a valley known as Collier's Lane is reached. This is part of the ancient London-Oxford road and is so called because it was used by Welsh colliers to take their coal to London. Turn sharp right onto this track (bridleway AR25), (briefly joining the reverse direction of Walk 3) and follow it for over half a mile, soon joining the edge of the wood. Now follow the track along the inside edge of Kingston Wood, ignoring all branching tracks, until you emerge by a double cottage at Parr's Common. Here join a farm road. In a few yards, on reaching a macadam road at the top of Kingston Hill, bear slightly left and follow the road to a staggered crossroads with the A40.

Turn right onto the A40 and follow it to a left-hand bend. Here fork right onto bridleway AR19 into Grove Wood (which, until 1824, was the course of the main road). After a quarter mile, just before a right-hand bend, turn right down a flight of steps, then continue steeply downhill. Where the path levels out, ignore a crossing track and descend into a gully. Continue straight on now for nearly a mile, leaving Grove Wood behind and crossing the Upper Icknield Way and the old railway. On reaching the B4009 by Woodway Farm, cross it and continue straight on along the road into Aston Rowant, ignoring various side turnings. Eventually the road bends to the right to Aston Rowant Church, built in the eleventh to fourteenth centuries.

At the road junction by the church, disregard the lane to the right leading to the attractive village green and instead, turn left into Church Lane, the oldest part of the village. Where the macadam surface ends, take bridleway AR15 straight on, ignoring a turning to the right and soon reaching a crossing lane, the Lower Icknield Way. Turn right onto this ancient road (AR8) and after half a mile, on reaching a ford, cross it by way of the footbridge on its left-hand side. After another quarter mile, cross the Kingston Stert road and go straight on, crossing a footbridge to the right of a further ford. After two more fields to the right (now on bridleway CR3), with the vast modern developments of Chinnor coming into view ahead, turn right onto bridleway CR2, an unfenced track between fields. Follow this, with Chinnor to the left and Kingston Blount to the right, for half a mile back to Crowell. On reaching the B4009, turn left along it, then, after about 30 yards, cross the road and take path CR4 through a kissing-gate, the churchyard and a lych-gate, back to the village green.

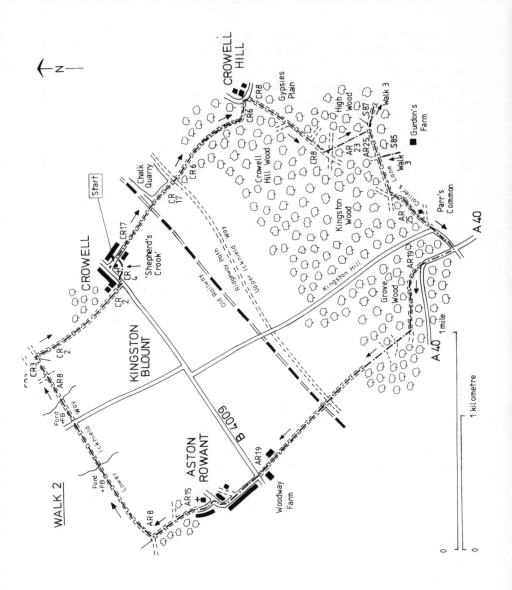

WALK 2

CROWELL

CROWELL HILL

Start

KINGSTON BLOUNT

ASTON ROWANT

N

CR3
CR2
AR8
Ford +FB
Icknield Way
Ford +FB
Lower
AR8
AR15
AR19
Woodway Farm
B4009
CR2
CR2
CR17
'Shepherd's Crook'
CR4
Chalk Quarry
CR17
CR6
CR6
CR8
CR8
Gypsies Plain
High Wood
S87
Walk 3
AR23
AR25
S85
Gurdon's Farm
Walk 3
Collier's Lane
Crowell Hill Wood
Kingston Wood
Kingston Hill
AR25
Parr's Common
Grove Wood
AR19
A40
A40
Ridgeway Path
Upper Icknield Way
Old Railway

0   1 kilometre
0   1 mile

WALK 3   Stokenchurch (North)

Length of Walk: 5.7 miles / 9.2 Km

Starting Point: 'King's Arms', Stokenchurch.

Grid Ref: SU760963

Maps: OS Landranger Sheet 165
      OS Explorer Sheet 171 (or old Sheet 3)
      OS Pathfinder Sheet 1137 (SU69/79)
      Chiltern Society FP Maps Nos. 7 & 14

How to get there / Parking: The starting point for this walk can be reached from the M40 by leaving it at Junction 5 (Stokenchurch) and taking the A40 into the centre of the village. There is a free public car park outside the 'King's Arms Hotel'.

Stokenchurch, which is spread along the A40 London–Oxford road on a ridgetop plateau about a mile from the escarpment and is one of the highest major settlements in the Chilterns, has the unfortunate reputation of being 'the ugly duckling' of the Chilterns. This may arise from its former role as a centre of the Bucks furniture industry with its consequent factories and timber yards, or from the extent to which it has been developed for housing since the coming of the M40. Nevertheless, the village can boast extensive, attractive, well-maintained village greens, where traditionally an annual horse fair used to be held on July 10th and 11th. The twelfth-century parish church, hidden behind the 'King's Arms', is quite sizeable when one considers that, until 1844, it was merely a chapel-of-ease for Aston Rowant and despite many renovations, it is well worth a visit. This is also the burial place of Hannah Ball (1734–1792), who was a friend of John Wesley and founded the first English Sunday school in High Wycombe in 1769.

For the walker, however, the chief attraction of Stokenchurch is that it is an ideal centre for exploring some of the finest Chiltern countryside including the Wormsley Valley, Penley Bottom, Radnage and the escarpment. This particular walk traverses the ridges and bottoms to the north of Stokenchurch, following Collier's Lane, the ancient Oxford road, for some distance and taking in parts of Radnage including Andridge with its fine views.

Starting from the forecourt of the 'King's Arms Hotel', an old coaching inn on the Oxford road, head west past several shops, cross a side road and bear half right across the green to its far corner. This was once the village bowling green and the magnificent lime trees on it are the remains of a circle. At the far corner, pass right of a large building with a rooflight, formerly the village bakehouse, and continue through an alleyway (path S86b) to reach a modern residential road. Turn right onto this road and follow it round to the left. At the end of the road, turn right onto footpath S86 between the houses to a gate and stile. Beyond the stile follow a hedge downhill. Where the hedge swings left, cross another stile and continue downhill between a hedge and a fence to a stile in the valley bottom. Cross this and bear half left across a steeply rising field. On reaching a hedge, follow it uphill to a stile into Stockfield Wood. Ignoring a fork to the right, take a winding path straight on downhill through the wood. At the bottom, turn left onto a track (path S85), soon leaving the wood by a stile. After another 70 yards, turn right following the left-hand side of a sporadic hedge uphill to a kissing-gate left of Gurdon's Farm. Go through this and bear half left across a small yard to a gate and stile. Here cross the stile and bear half right, joining a right hand hedge and following it downhill to a stile beside a New Zealand (barbed-wire) gate at the Oxfordshire boundary leading into Kingston Wood.

Having crossed the stile, you come to Collier's Lane, (bridleway AR25), the ancient road from London to Oxford which was replaced by the modern A40 through Stokenchurch. Turn right onto this track which hugs the valley bottom (briefly joining the reverse direction of Walk 2). Ignoring all branching tracks, follow this ancient road (soon as bridleway S87) through the woods for nearly a mile, eventually re-emerging into the open. A few yards beyond this, where the valley meets another in which Hallbottom Farm can be seen to the right, turn left onto a farm road (still S87 and Collier's Lane) and follow it along the valley floor for another two-thirds of a mile.

On nearing Pophley's Farm to your left, look out for a signposted path to your right. Having joined the Chiltern Way, after a further 70 yards bear half left onto path CR10, crossing two fields diagonally to a rail-stile at the foot of a screening bank. Now cross this stile and bear right along the foot of the bank then turn left onto a farm track. After 20 yards turn right through a hedge gap leading to Grange Farm Road. Here go through a hedge gap opposite onto path RA16 and continue straight on across a field, climbing at first gradually, then more steeply, making for an electricity pole in the hedge ahead. On reaching the hedge, turn left along it. At a gap in the corner of the field, first turn round to look at the extensive view across the valley towards Stokenchurch. Now go through the gap and turn right over a stile, then cross a paddock diagonally to gates and a stile in its far corner. Cross this stile, the drive to Andridge Farm and a stile by gates opposite. Now turn right onto a second drive (path RA17), keeping left of a bungalow. Where the drive forks, take a concrete track straight on emerging into a field. Here a magnificent view opens out ahead, of Radnage Bottom flanked by Bledlow Ridge to the left and the Radnage Common ridge to the right. In the distance on West Wycombe Hill is St. Lawrence's Church, a thirteenth-century church extensively rebuilt in 1763 by Francis Lord le Despencer who added to its tower the golden ball for which it is famous.

Leaving the Chiltern Way here, bear half right onto path RA14, which normally *follows a crop break, heading towards some farm buildings in the valley below. Soon you join a right-hand hedge and follow it downhill to Horseshoe Road. Some way down the hill, the church which comes into view to the left is that of Radnage, built in the early thirteenth century. Turn right onto the road and follow it downhill past the picturesque 'Three Horseshoes' into Bennett End. Where the road forks, go right and by an attractive gabled sixteenth-century cottage, cross a crossroads and take bridleway RA22 straight on towards a hill. At the foot of a steep slope, where a large house appears ahead, follow bridleway RA21 round to the left. At a fork, take path RA23 straight on, climbing gradually and curving to the right. When a view opens out to the left, continue straight on between a hedge and a fence, crossing a ladder stile and eventually emerging on a road in grandiose-sounding Radnage City.

Turn right onto this road called City Road and follow it for a quarter mile, passing the 'Crown'. When you reach the driveway to Pophley's (bridleway S76) at a sharp left-hand bend, fork right onto it. Where the drive turns right, take path S75 straight on, crossing a stile into a hedged path leading to another stile. Having crossed this, bear slightly left across a field to reach the right-hand end of a hedge. Here turn round to look at the extensive view before continuing straight on along a winding grass track across fields towards Stokenchurch. After about half a mile, by the far end of a left-hand hedge, leave the track and continue straight on across a field to reach a hedge gap where path S75 becomes enclosed between a hedge and a fence. After 250 yards it turns left, follows the perimeter of a playing field and continues to a metal kissing-gate. Here ignore a path branching to the left and go straight on to a road junction, where you bear slightly right into George Road. At a fork in the road, go left, then at a T-junction, turn left again. At the next road junction, turn right into Littlewood and just past house No. 52, turn left onto a macadam path leading to Lower Church Street. On reaching the road, turn right, then immediately left to emerge onto Stokenchurch village green where the 'King's Arms' is to your right.

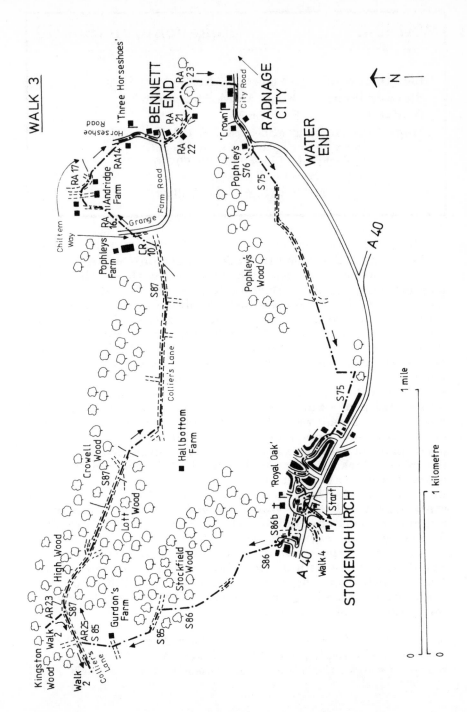

WALK 3

23

WALK 4: Stokenchurch (South)

Length of Walk: 5.4 miles / 8.7 Km
Starting Point: 'King's Arms', Stokenchurch.
Grid Ref: SU760963
Maps: OS Landranger Sheets 165 & 175
        OS Explorer Sheet 171 (or old Sheet 3)
        OS Pathfinder Sheet 1137 (SU69/79)
        Chiltern Society FP Map No. 14
How to get there / Parking: See Walk 3.

Stokenchurch, described in Walk 3, is not only a large village but also a large parish and together with much of the neighbouring parish of Ibstone, it was only transferred from Oxfordshire to Buckinghamshire during the nineteenth century. In its south-western corner is a sizeable part of the Wormsley Valley, most of which belongs to the Wormsley Estate. This Estate was for over 400 years in the hands of one family, the Scropes and later, through female succession, the Fanes. It is thanks to them that no public road has ever been established through this beautiful valley and, in consequence, its natural peace and serenity have been preserved. In 1984, however, the Estate was sold to a holding company representing John Paul Getty and since then large amounts of money have been spent on renovating the farms and cottages and not least Wormsley Park, its manor house of Palladian, eighteenth-century appearance but concealing some much older fabric. Extensive work has also been carried out on clearing and replanting the Estate's storm-ravaged woodlands, but much remains to be done and it will be many years before their former glory has been restored.

This walk, to the south of Stokenchurch, takes you by way of Studdridge Farm with its fine views to the south towards the Thames Valley and beyond to Ibstone's airy hilltop common, before descending into and exploring the Wormsley Valley and returning to Stokenchurch.

Starting from the forecourt of the 'King's Arms Hotel', take the Chiltern Way crossing the A40 and keeping right of the 'Four Horseshoes', take a road across the green to Coopers Court Road.

Follow this downhill, crossing Slade Road and taking a farm road (path S27) straight on to the tunnel under the M40. At the far end of this, fork right onto the drive to Coopers Court Farm and cross a stile to the left of a gate into a field. Bear slightly left across the field to another stile left of the farmhouse and a large tree. Turn left over the stile and follow a cattle drive alongside a hedge. It may be necessary at one or two points to go through New Zealand (barbed-wire) gates which are placed across the path to route cattle to the required destination. To avoid inconvenience to the farmer, these should be left as they are found. At the end of the cattle drive, go through another New Zealand gate and follow the right-hand hedge downhill to a footbridge and stile into Bissomhill Shaw. Cross these and follow the path uphill by a fence through this belt of trees to a stile and gate, then follow a right-hand hedge uphill to a stile at the top. Having crossed this, take path S28, bearing half left across a field to the left-hand nearside corner of a group of trees concealing two ponds. Follow the left side of this group to the far end, then bear half right across the field to a gate and stile onto the drive to Studdridge Farm.

Join the drive and follow it past the farmhouse. Where the drive turns left, continue straight on to a gate and kissing-gate between two barns. Here a magnificent view opens out towards the distant Thames Valley. Go through the kissing-gate, then follow a right-hand fence and hedge to a gate and stile in a crossing hedge. Having crossed the stile, follow a right-hand hedge and line of trees crossing a further stile by a gate into a plantation until the hedge swings to the left. Here turn right into an area of scrubland and follow a waymarked path (still S28) through it to reach a field. Now turn right and follow the edge of Commonhill Wood downhill to a hedge gap in the corner of the field into Hartmoor Wood. Leaving the Chiltern Way, just inside the wood turn left and follow a winding waymarked path uphill for a third of a mile through self-regenerating woodland, ignoring crossing or branching tracks. On nearing a field ahead, join a track and follow it straight on, disregarding branching tracks, until you pass through a gap by a gate and follow a rough lane (now on path I17) to reach a road at Ibstone Common.

Turn right onto this road and follow it for some 200 yards. Where scrubland begins on the common, bear half left onto ill-defined bridleway I20, passing right of the first clump of bushes and then skirting a left-hand copse to reach the well-defined bridleway I18 near a large pond at the back of the common. Turn left onto this bridleway, rejoining the Chiltern Way and follow it for about 80 yards, then, at an obvious fork, go right onto bridleway S7a, passing between hedges into Great Wood. Just inside the wood, keep left and follow the obvious bridleway through storm-ravaged woodland for about 200 yards, eventually entering a deep descending gully. Some 200 yards down this gully, turn left onto waymarked path S21, crossing the bank, then dropping steeply and soon emerging into a field.

Here a view opens out over the tranquil southern end of the Wormsley Valley with Northend on a distant ridge. Turn right and follow a fence and sporadic hedge downhill to a crossing hedge. Here cross a stile and leaving the Chiltern Way again, turn right onto fenced bridleway S7. Now follow this bridleway, which forms the spine of the rights of way network in the valley, straight on along the valley bottom, soon passing through a spinney and joining a grassy track. Go straight on along this beside a right-hand hedge, then, where the hedge ends, take a fenced farm road straight on, looking out for a view of the Wormsley Park house through the trees to your left. On reaching a bend in a macadam farm road, join it and follow it straight on for over a quarter mile.

On nearing the hamlet of Wellground, ignore a fork to your left, then, just past a thatched cottage at a junction of farm roads and tracks, fork half left onto a woodland track (bridleway S8). Having passed the back of a cottage, take a track straight on climbing gently through scrubby woodland. After some 300 yards you take bridleway L19 straight on along a track through storm-ravaged woodland for about a third of a mile until a waymarked crossing path is reached where you meet the route of Walk 5. Here turn right onto path L20 and follow this over a rise, then descend to a stile out of the wood. Cross this and resume your previous direction, following the outside edge of the wood at first, then continuing straight on downhill to a stile into South Remlets Wood at the Bucks county boundary. Just inside the wood, fork half left onto path S3 and, ignoring a crossing path to Reeds Farm, follow a winding waymarked path uphill until you emerge onto a rough track (path S2) at the far corner of the wood. Join the track and follow it for a quarter mile, crossing a field and continuing along a lane, until you reach a road. Cross the road and continue straight on along path S2 to Mill Road. Turn left onto this and just before its end, turn right into Green Lane. Now follow this for nearly half a mile, crossing the M40 by a footbridge and passing the village allotments and cricket field to your left, until you reach the A40 near the starting point.

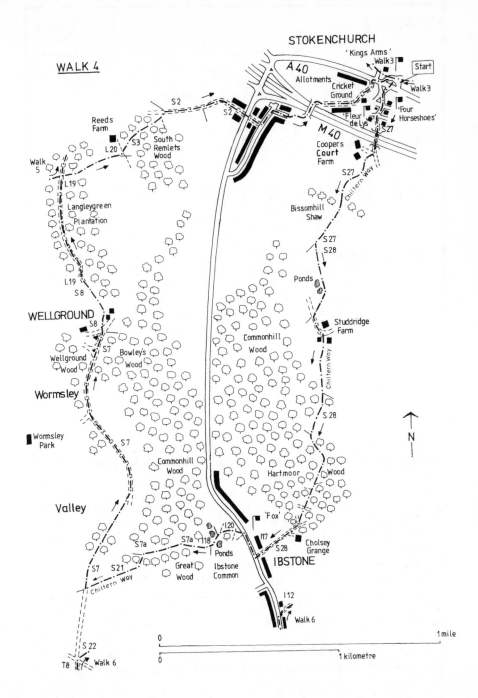

WALK 4

STOKENCHURCH

'Kings Arms' Walk 3
Start
Walk 3

A 40
Allotments
Cricket Ground
'Four Horseshoes'
'Fleur de Lys'
S 27

Reeds Farm
South Remlets Wood
L 20
S 3
S 2
S 2

M 40
Coopers Court Farm
S 27

Walk 5
L 19
Langleygreen Plantation
Chiltern Way
Bissomhill Shaw
S 27
S 28

L 19
S 8

Ponds

WELLGROUND
S 8
S 7
Bowley's Wood
Commonhill Wood
Studdridge Farm
Wellground Wood
Wormsley
Chiltern Way
S 28

Wormsley Park
S 7

Commonhill Wood
Hartmoor
Wood
N

Valley

'Fox'
I 20
I 17
S 7a
S 7a
I 18
Cholsey Grange
S 7
S 21
Ponds
S 28
IBSTONE
Great Wood
Ibstone Common
Chiltern Way

I 12
Walk 6

S 22
T 8   Walk 6

0   1 mile
0   1 kilometre

27

WALK 5:   Lewknor
(Cowleaze Wood Picnic Area)

Length of Walk: (A)   10.9 miles / 17.5 Km
                     (B)   4.7 miles / 7.6 Km
                     (C)   8.4 miles / 13.5 Km

Starting Point: Vehicular entrance to Cowleaze Wood
                     Picnic Area.

Grid Ref: SU726956

Maps: OS Landranger Sheets 165 & (A/C only) 175
         OS Explorer Sheet 171 (or old Sheet 3)
         OS Pathfinder Sheet 1137 (SU69/79)
         (B and parts of A/C only) Chiltern Society FP map No. 9

How to get there / Parking: Cowleaze Wood Picnic Area,
some 9 miles west of High Wycombe, may be reached by
leaving the M40 at Junction 5 (Stokenchurch) and taking
the A40 towards Oxford. After two-thirds of a mile, turn
left onto the road signposted to Christmas Common and
follow it for 1.6 miles, then turn left into the picnic area.

Notes: Heavy nettle growth may be encountered on paths PY9
and SH3 on Walks A and C in the summer months.

Cowleaze Wood Picnic Area, at the top of Bald Hill above
Lewknor, was established by the Forestry Commission in the
1960s as part of their policy of promoting public access to their
woodlands in order to make proper provision for a popular
existing picnic spot. For the Chiltern Society, this wood is of
special significance as path L23, which had been obliterated
by a plantation, was the first path clearance job the Society's
Rights of Way Group ever tackled. Today this is hard to
imagine as this path now forms the heavily-used hub of a
popular network of paths in the wood.

    All three variants of this walk offer a selection of superb
views in what is one of the scenically most spectacular and
attractive parts of the Chilterns which enjoys a justified
popularity with walkers. Walks A and B both commence by
traversing the wood to explore the upper reaches of the
Wormsley Valley, which, with its wooded slopes and freedom
from public roads, remains a haven of peace and beauty. You

then descend Beacon Hill with its panoramic views across the Oxfordshire Plain before Walk B reascends to the picnic area. Walk C first descends the escarpment with some superb views to meet Walk A at Lewknor before both explore the quiet country at the foot of the escarpment with small villages steeped in history and fine views of the hills and finally return up the side of Shirburn Hill to the picnic area.

Starting from the vehicular entrance to Cowleaze Wood Picnic Area, **Walks A and B** head straight into the wood. At a crossways, pass right of a gate ahead and follow a wide track straight on soon joining path L23. At a crossways under a power-line, take the waymarked path straight on for half a mile ignoring all crossing or branching paths until you emerge into a field with a fine view of the Wormsley Valley ahead. Now take path S12 straight on passing just left of the first telegraph pole, then continuing downhill (now on L23 again) to a hedge gap leading to bridleway L29. Turn left onto this and follow it to a hedge to your right. Just past this hedge turn right onto path L23, crossing a stile and continuing downhill and up again past Lower Vicar's Farm to a stile by a hawthorn tree. Cross this and bear half left across a field to a stile into a wood. Now follow a winding waymarked path uphill to reach a crossways where you meet the route of Walk 4. Here turn left onto bridleway L19 and follow its waymarked course straight on for over a third of a mile to reach the M40 deer fence. Now bear half left following this fence to pass through a bridlegate. Just beyond this gate, turn left and follow the deer fence up an embankment. Where this fence ends, turn right up the bank and step over the crash-barrier to reach the Christmas Common road.

Turn right onto this road, crossing the M40 bridge and continuing along its verge for 200 yards. Now turn left onto path L16 up some steps to a stile into Grant's Plantation. Here go straight on to reach gates leading in a few yards to the old Christmas Common road. Turn left onto this and follow it to a left-hand bend, then turn right through a gap by a gate onto path L12 into Little London Wood. At a fork just inside the wood, go left leaving the waymarked path and taking an English Nature permissive path along the inside edge of the wood. (From here to the Upper Icknield Way the route follows permissive paths which can be closed at any time. Should this occur, an alternative route via public rights of way is indicated on the plan.) After a third of a mile go through a squeeze-stile by a gate and fork left onto a path up a series of steps to join a fence. Follow this along the side of Beacon Hill with views of the Oxfordshire Plain starting to open out to the right, then turning left, then right, then left again to cross the face of the hill. Now bear right down some steps to pass through a kissing-gate, then follow an obvious path straight on downhill to enter a sunken way by a single yew tree. On rounding the hill you re-emerge from the gully and continue past a small copse to three steps down to a stile. Do not cross this, but turn sharp right and follow a grassy track around the foot of the hill for over a third of a mile, eventually bearing left and dropping to cross a stile by a gate onto the ancient Upper Icknield Way and modern Ridgeway Path (L11).

Walk A turns right onto this green road and follows it into a copse then turns left onto waymarked path L10, dropping through the copse into a field. Here follow a left-hand fence straight on to the fence of an M40 slip road, then turn right and follow it to a rail-stile leading to the junction of the slip road and B4009. Cross the B4009 here and turn left along the back of a wooden fence on its verge. After 50 yards turn right over a rail-stile onto path L10 and bear half left across a field to a gate in the far corner by the M40 fence. Now follow this fence to cross a stile by a gate at the end of a road. Cross this road and take a fenced path straight on, turning left under the M40 and turning left again to reach the end of Lewknor village street. Turn right onto this road and follow it into the village to reach the gates of Lewknor School and Church, through which you turn right. Now omit the next two paragraphs.

Walk B turns left onto this green road passing under the M40 at a point where a Roman cemetery was discovered during construction work and reaching a crossing macadam road called Hill Road. Turn left onto this passing Hill Farm. Where the macadam ends, bear half right following the attractive chalky continuation uphill, passing through scrubby woodlands with ancient yew trees and eventually levelling out to reach the Christmas Common road. Cross this to enter the picnic area and turn right onto a wide track parallel to the road which leads you back to your starting point.

Walk C also starts from the vehicular entrance to the picnic area and follows it into the wood. At a crossways turn left along a track parallel to the Christmas Common road. Where the vehicle track ends, turn left crossing the road, then turn right through a former gateway into fenced bridleway L31 which soon widens into the old road. By a large grassy mound partially blocking this road, turn left through a hedge gap onto path L15, a winding grassy track which leads you downhill with fine views. Near the foot of the hill follow the track round to the right, then turn left over a stile by a gate onto path L14, a grassy track leading you to the end of the macadamed part of Hill Road by Hill Farm. Turn right onto this road and follow it for half a mile to reach the B4009. Cross this and turn left along its verge, then by a bus pull-in turn sharp right down a concrete path into a village street at Lewknor. Follow this to the crossroads by 'Ye Olde Leathern

Bottel', then turn right into High Street passing Townpool with its spring and watercress beds. On reaching the gates of Lewknor School and Church, turn left through them joining **Walk A**.

Walks A & C go through the lychgate into the churchyard, then fork left off the macadam path onto path L9, a grassy path passing left of the twelfth-century church with a fourteenth-century chancel and fifteenth-century tower to a kissing-gate at the back of the churchyard. Go through this and continue straight on between barns at Church Farm to a stile, then bear half left across two fields to reach a footbridge. Cross this and bear half right across the next field to a gate in front of a brick-and-flint barn which leads you to Weston Road. Turn right onto this quiet country lane and follow it straight on for two-thirds of a mile, passing Moor Court which was rebuilt in the eighteenth century but retains large sections of its mediaeval moat, to reach the tiny village of South Weston with its hillside church rebuilt in 1864 but incorporating features of its fourteenth-century predecessor.

Here pass Manor Farm with its substantial eighteenth-century brick-and-flint farmhouse, then by the village postbox turn left into a cul-de-sac road. At the end of the road turn right onto path L30, a grassy fenced track and follow it bearing left and passing the Old Rectory with its attractive artificial lake. Near the far end of its grounds, ignore a branching track to the left and go straight on to the end of the track by a footbridge. Turn left over this bridge then turn right and follow a right-hand fence beside a stream at first to a hedge gap and stile at the far end of the field. Cross the stile and turn left onto path SH2, the Oxfordshire Way, following a left-hand hedge uphill to a corner of the field. Here turn right and follow a left-hand hedge with Model Farm to your left. Built in 1857 for the contemporary Earl of Macclesfield, this farm with its covered ways and yards and steam-driven machinery incorporated all the latest developments in farming technology and at the time attracted visitors from all over the country. On reaching the end of a belt of trees, turn left through a gate, then right over a stile and follow the edge of the tree belt to a gate and stile onto a farm road. Cross this road and a stile by a gate opposite then bear half left across a field to cross a stile in the far corner. Now go through the left-hand of two gates and continue straight on across the next field to cross a stile in the far corner of the field. Here turn right into a green lane (the ancient Lower Icknield Way). Through the trees to your left, you may at some point glimpse Shirburn Castle, the only intact castle left in the Chiltern area, built in 1377 and home to the Earls of Macclesfield since 1716. At a junction of tracks wiggle slightly to the right crossing a culvert and a stile by a gate onto bridleway PY7. Now follow this straight on, passing a nineteenth-century lodge, to reach Pyrton village street.

Pyrton, at the crossroads of the Lower Icknield Way and equally ancient Knightsbridge Lane (or Ruggeway), is believed to be a particularly early settlement and it was at the village church that John Hampden, a Parliamentarian leader in the Civil War, married Elizabeth Symeon of the nearby Elizabethan manor house in 1619.

Turn left onto the road then immediately right through the gate of a seventeenth-century cottage, keeping close to the cottage wall to enter fenced path PY9. Go straight along this crossing two stiles, then follow the left-hand fence through a paddock to cross a further stile. Here bear half right across a field to reach a farm road by a stile. Cross this, then bear half right across a paddock to go through a gate just left of its far corner. Now turn left and take path PY8 beside a left-hand stream to a stile by a cottage into the end of a rough lane. Take this lane straight on past Pyrton Church, rebuilt in 1855 but retaining certain features of its twelfth-century predecessor, to a bend in a road. Now follow this road straight on for three-quarters of a mile, looking out for a view of Shirburn Castle through the left-hand hedge, crossing the B4009 and passing the ruins of Watlington Station, the terminus of the Watlington Branch Line opened in 1872 and closed in 1957. Where the public road ends, take bridleway PY4 straight on along its private continuation for two-thirds of a mile crossing the Upper Icknield Way/Ridgeway Path. Some 40 yards beyond the start of an area of scrub to the left, turn left onto path PY16, a grassy track through the scrub which winds its way across the foot of Pyrton Hill with its ancient yew trees and fine views of Shirburn Hill ahead and the Oxfordshire Plain to your left. After some 200 yards by a large clump of yew trees to your right, leave this track and take a worn path straight on. On entering Shirburn Wood, you soon reach a junction of tracks. Here take waymarked path SH3 straight on beside a fence along the edge of the wood. By a gate in the fence turn right onto a waymarked track, then by the corner of a field turn left onto a crossing track. After the woodland has given way to scrub, at a fork take a narrower path straight on soon wiggling to the left and following a fence. Where the fence turns left at the foot of Shirburn Hill, bear half-right following a worn path up the side of the hill turning round for a fine view towards Wittenham Clumps before passing through a belt of trees near the top. At its far side, cross a stile and go straight on, heading just left of a row of cypresses, to reach a stile onto the Christmas Common Road. Turn left onto this and opposite signposted path L17 to the left, take a path through a gap in the right-hand fence into Cowleaze Wood which soon reaches the main track through the picnic area. Now go straight on for your starting point.

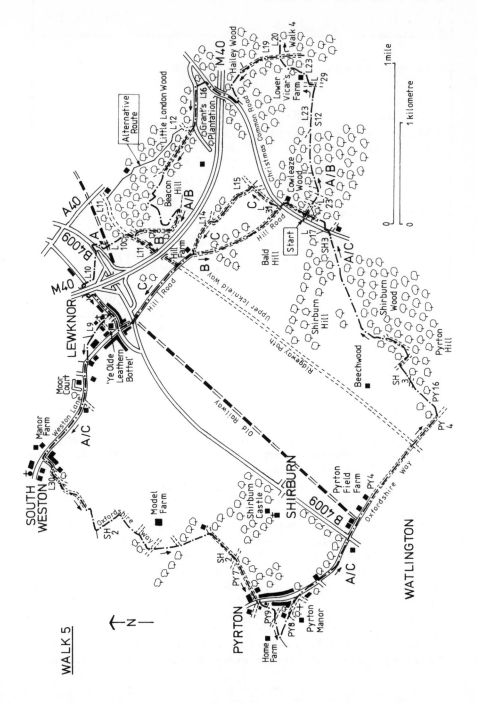

WALK 5

33

WALK 6:   Northend

Length of walk: (A) 6.0 miles / 9.7 Km
                       (B) 4.0 miles / 6.5 Km
Starting Point: 'White Hart', Northend.
Grid Ref: SU734924
Maps: OS Landranger Sheet 175
            OS Explorer Sheet 171 (or old Sheet 3)
            OS Pathfinder Sheet 1137 (SU69/79)
            Chiltern Society FP Maps (A) Nos. 9, 11 & 14
                                      (B) No. 9 only

How to get there / Parking: Northend, 8 miles west of High
    Wycombe, may be reached by leaving the M40 at Junction
    5 (Stokenchurch) and taking the A40 towards Oxford for
    two-thirds of a mile. Now turn left onto the road to
    Christmas Common. At Christmas Common, fork left onto
    the Northend road for 1.3 miles to a road junction near
    Northend Pond, where you bear right for the 'White Hart'
    and park along the edge of the common. Do not use the
    pub car park without the landlord's permission, block
    driveways or park more than 15 feet from the road.

Northend, with its scattered cottages spread unevenly around
its extensive heathy and, in parts, wooded common, is
justifiably popular with both picnickers and walkers owing to
its attractive setting and the superb Chiltern views which can
be obtained from surrounding footpaths. Although the village
now straddles the county boundary, its name derives from its
location at the northern end of the Buckinghamshire parish of
Turville.

Both alternative walks explore part of the remote country
near the Oxfordshire border which, with its steep-sided
valleys flanked by beautiful beechwoods, can be described as
one of the finest and most unspoilt areas of the Buckinghamshire Chilterns. From Northend, both alternatives lead you
into the depths of the Wormsley Valley, which is singularly
remote in that it contains no public roads, before you climb to
Ibstone's lofty ridge. Walk A then continues into another
spectacular valley beyond before both routes return by way of
the upper reaches of Turville's celebrated valley to Northend.

Starting from the 'White Hart' at Northend, take the right-hand of two roads across the common northwards to a fork by the large duckpond. Here fork right, crossing another road and taking bridleway T8, a rough track, straight on. Ignore a forking track to the left and pass through some gates, then follow a winding hedged lane for a quarter mile, ignoring field entrances and short branching tracks and descending gradually with occasional views through the right-hand hedge towards the Turville Valley. At one point a superb view opens out ahead of the Wormsley Valley with the Stokenchurch Telecom Tower in the background. Now continue straight on downhill and where the main track turns left into a copse, fork right into a sunken hedged lane dropping into the Wormsley Valley.

On reaching a farm road, cross it and bear half right over a stile onto path S22, crossing a field diagonally to a stile at a slight bend in the edge of Hale Wood. Cross this stile and take the waymarked path into the wood, after a few yards turning right. Soon the path bears left and joins a track which you follow to the far side of the wood. Here bear slightly left across a narrow field to enter Great Wood, then follow the waymarked track uphill through this severely storm-damaged beechwood. The steepest part of the hill you ascend by a terraced timber track, then, where it forks, turn sharp left. After a further 40 yards, turn right onto a waymarked path which soon emerges into a field. Go straight on across this field, passing a pond to your right, to reach path I22 between garden hedges leading to a cottage drive. Now turn right down this drive to reach Grays Lane, Ibstone opposite a cottage called Hell Corner Farm. Legend has it that this name arose because attempts in the past to build a church on the site had failed due to the structure repeatedly falling down and this was thought to be the work of the devil!

Turn left into Grays Lane, then turn immediately right across a strip of grass and the macadam drive to Hell Corner Farm to enter Parsonage Wood. Just inside this wood, **Walk B** forks right and follows the waymarked path I4 downhill. At the bottom, by the corner of a right-hand field, turn right and climb gradually through the wood for a quarter mile to reach another waymarked junction where you fork right again and rejoin Walk A. Now omit the next two paragraphs.

Walk A, however, forks left just inside the wood onto path I1, descending gradually to a stile in the valley bottom. Now cross this stile and follow the outside edge of the wood, later a hedge uphill through two fields, then continue straight on between hedges and fences to reach the ridgetop road along which most of Ibstone's scattered houses and cottages are situated. Turn left onto this road, then, at a slight left-hand bend, turn right onto a gravel drive (path I12).

After the gravel surface ends, take a green lane straight on downhill until you enter a young plantation, where fine views open out down the valley to your right towards Fingest. Now follow the left-hand hedge straight on through the plantation and a field to the bottom corner of the field where you go straight on into woodland known as Twigside Bottom. Here follow a track straight on downhill, ignoring two branching tracks to your right and two to your left, to a T-junction of tracks where you turn left, disregard a forking track to the left and soon reach a track junction by an old gatepost.

At this junction, turn sharp right onto path I14a, later LE45 then I14, and follow this track along the valley bottom for half a mile, ignoring one crossing track and reaching a second. Here cross this track and take the left-hand of two tracks for some 100 yards. Now turn right onto bridleway I2, crossing the other track and winding through a mature plantation until you reach a wide forest track. Turn left onto this track passing a field to your left, then, by the corner of a garden hedge, fork right (now on footpath I2) leaving the track, following the back of a lawn and soon entering Grove Wood. Inside the wood, follow the waymarked path straight on, crossing a track and continuing to a stile. Cross this stile and continue uphill to the corner of a hedge where you pass through a hedge gap and follow a right-hand fence uphill with a view to your left of the characteristic Chiltern brick-and-flint village school with its bellcot and the eighteenth-century Ibstone House, former home of the authoress Dame Rebecca West. Now cross a stile and follow a fenced path to the ridgetop road at Ibstone. Having crossed this, take path I2 straight on through gates and over a stile into a field where you follow the left-hand fence to a further stile into Parsonage Wood.

Inside the wood turn left at a path junction onto path I4, rejoining **Walk B**, and follow this path along the contours of the hill for nearly half a mile, entering a plantation and ignoring a branching path to the left. On reaching a second branching path to the left into Ibstone churchyard, if wishing to visit the little twelfth-century church with its ancient yew tree, turn left; otherwise, continue straight on for a few yards, then turn right, dropping steeply across a track and a stile into a field by an ancient stone Wormsley Estate cattle trough where a fine view opens out over the Turville Valley. Now turn left and follow the edge of the wood, later a fence downhill to a stile. Cross this stile and continue straight on downhill to a stile leading into a corner of Turville Wood. Inside this storm-ravaged wood, follow the waymarked path, crossing a concrete road, joining bridleway I21 which merges from the left and reaching a fork. Here bear left onto bridleway T28 and follow it to reach a road called Holloway Lane by the gates of the Wormsley Estate.

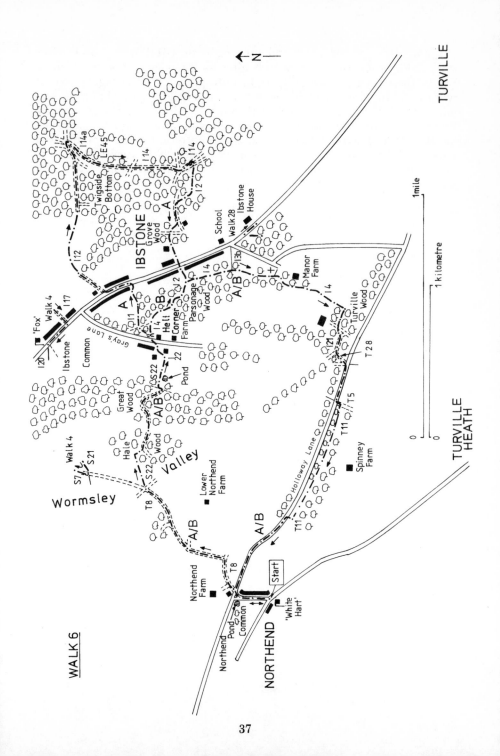

WALK 6

Wormsley

IBSTONE

NORTHEND

TURVILLE

TURVILLE HEATH

Start

'White Hart'

Northend Common
Northend Pond
Northend Farm

T8
A/B
A/B

Lower Northend Farm
Hale Wood
Valley
Great Wood
A/B
CS22
Pond

Walk 4
S7 S21

S22
22

Holloway Lane

Spinney Farm
T11
T5
T11
T28

Turville Wood
T21
T14

Manor Farm

A/B
Walk 28
Ibstone House
School

Parsonage Wood
Hell Corner Farm
14
11
A
B
I14
I12
A/B

Gray's Lane
Ibstone Common
Walk 4
'Fox'
I20
I17

Grove Wood
A

I12
I114a
LE45
I14
Twigside Bottom
I12

37

Ignore this private road and turn right into Holloway Lane. After some 250 yards, turn left onto bridleway T5, signposted to Spinney Farm, then turn immediately right onto path T11, the right-hand of two branching tracks, which leads you to a stile. Cross this stile and follow the left-hand fence uphill through woodland with views of the Wormsley Valley through the trees to your right until you reach another stile. Having crossed this, continue to follow the waymarked path straight on until it rejoins Holloway Lane. Now turn left into the lane and follow it to the road junction by Northend Pond, then turn left for your starting point.

WALK 7:   Turville Heath

Length of Walk: 5.6 miles / 9.1 Km

Starting Point: Entrance to car park at Turville Heath.

Grid Ref: SU745909

Maps: OS Landranger Sheet 175
OS Explorer Sheet 171 (or old Sheet 3)
OS Pathfinder Sheets 1137 (SU69/79) & 1156 (SU68/78)
Chiltern Society FP Map No. 9

How to get there / Parking: Turville Heath, 5.3 miles north
of Henley-on-Thames, may be reached from the town by
taking the A4130 towards Oxford for 1.5 miles. At the far
end of a long straight known as The Fairmile, turn right
onto the Assendons and Stonor road. After 3 miles, just
beyond Stonor, fork right again for Turville Heath and
follow this road for 1.3 miles to a further fork. Here go
right and at a crossroads, continue straight on, then
immediately turn left into a small unofficial car park.

Notes: Heavy nettle growth may be encountered on path
PS9 in the summer months.

Turville Heath, which, as its name suggests, is a heathy upland
common of Turville parish, also has a number of scattered
cottages and two of the three large mansions in the parish.
Turville Grange, an imposing Georgian mansion, has been
noted in recent years as the home of Jacqueline Kennedy's
sister and later a member of the Ford family, while Turville
Park, an older house to the west of Turville Heath, is where
the exiled French royalist army commander, General
Dumouriez, died in 1823.

The walk first leads you across the heath, which is popular
with picnickers and through Turville Park on its upland
plateau before you reach one of the Chilterns' most beautiful
valleys, where Rolls Bottom and Pishill Bottom converge to
form the Stonor or Assendon valley. In some ways, this valley
is typical of the Chilterns with mostly arable fields on the
lower slopes and attractive beechwoods capping the hills, but
its distinction lies in having been largely spared the ravages of
twentieth-century development and the fact that it contains

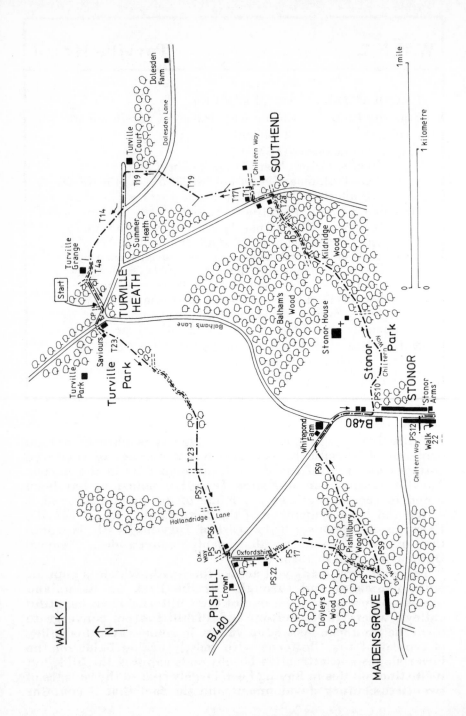

WALK 7

←N—

40

Stonor Park with its medieval manor house surrounded by an extensive deer park. As well as passing through Stonor Park, the walks also visits Pishill and skirts Maidensgrove with fine views and pleasant woodland alternating in quick succession, before reaching the hilltop hamlet of Southend with its superb views to the east and returning to Turville Heath.

Starting from the entrance to the unofficial car park, turn right onto the priority road and at a T-junction, cross the Northend road noticing a fine avenue of ancient limes to your right and take path T23 along the drive to 'Saviours', a small late-Victorian church now converted into a private house. By its gate, fork left to a small gate into a field forming part of Turville Park, then bear slightly right to a gate followed by a stile. Now keep straight on across two fields, crossing another stile and passing right of a wooded pit to reach a kissing-gate leading onto a fenced track. Turn right onto this track (still T23) and where it emerges into a field, follow the right-hand fence and belt of trees to a gap into the next field. Here wide views open out ahead of the Stonor valley backed by Lambridge Wood (above Henley) and, on a clear day, the distant Hog's Back and to the right towards Christmas Common and Northend. Now follow the right-hand fence and a tree belt straight on. On reaching a small copse, bear slightly right through it to cross a stile. Now take a grassy track straight on downhill to a hedge gap right of a Dutch barn. Continue straight on through this gap, here entering Oxfordshire, and take path PS7, keeping left of a slight bank and following it uphill to reach Hollandridge Lane on the crest of the ridge. Cross this Saxon road and take path PS6 straight on, following a left-hand hedge downhill to a stile. Having crossed this, take a fenced path straight on past a former farm to a stile leading onto the Oxfordshire Way. Turn left onto this track (path PS5) and follow it to the B480 at Pishill, which originally meant 'hill where peas grow'.

Turn right onto this road, then turn immediately left into Church Lane (signposted 'Oxfordshire Way') and follow it uphill past the Norman church with a fine view to your left towards Stonor Park. Where the road ends, bear slightly left onto bridleway PS22, a fenced track and follow it past a garden. Where the track forks, take bridleway PS17 (the Oxfordshire Way) straight on through a hedge gap and follow the left-hand hedge downhill and up again into Pishillbury Wood. Just inside the wood, cross a track and follow the waymarked bridleway uphill. At the top continue straight on with a field visible to your right. Just before reaching some houses to your right at Maidensgrove, described in 1940 by the well-known Chiltern writer, H J Massingham, as 'perhaps the most remote hamlet in all the Chilterns', turn left onto path PS9 and follow it for half a mile through this wood rich in bluebells. Eventually the path leaves the wood and continues downhill between hedges to the B480 road. Turn right onto this road and follow it swinging right and passing the turning for Turville Heath and the lodge gates of Stonor Park with lions rampant on the gateposts to reach a kissing-gate in the deer park fence.

Now, joining the Chiltern Way, turn left through this kissing-gate onto the well-worn, path PS10 through the park with its sizeable herd of fallow deer and follow its winding course for three-quarters of a mile to reach a further kissing-gate into Kildridge Wood on the far side of the park. On the way, this path gives you a grandstand view of Stonor House and the adjoining chapel. Both house and chapel date from about 1280 and have, for all that time, been the home of the Stonor family (since 1838 the Barons Camoys), but, over the years, both house and chapel have been subject to considerable alterations with the result that the house now has a Georgian appearance. Despite the reformation, the family have always remained staunch Catholics and secret hiding places were constructed to conceal such fugitives as Edmund Campion and even today the chapel is a centre for Catholics over a wide area.

On leaving the park, continue straight on through Kildridge Wood to a junction of tracks. Here bear half right, following a woodland track uphill and where it levels out, continue straight on (now on path T2a and once again in Bucks) until you reach a road by an old lodge at Southend. Turn left onto this road and after some 150 yards turn right onto a concrete road along the edge of Southend Common (bridleway T1). Just before reaching the back of the common, leaving the Chiltern Way, turn left over a stile onto path T17 where you obtain a fine view across the hilltops with Turville Court ahead and Cobstone Windmill half to the right. Now follow a left-hand fence straight on to a gate and stile. Cross this stile and take path T19, bearing half right to a stile in the valley at the bottom end of a hedge. Cross this stile, Dolesden Lane and another stile opposite, then climb steeply (still on T19), following a right-hand hedge, then the edge of Home Wood, to double gates and a stile leading to a road by Turville Court. Turn left onto this road and follow it to a road junction, then turn right over a stile onto path T14. Now bear half left across the field, aiming just left of a twin-trunked ash tree to join a hedge, then bear slightly left and follow this hedge to two stiles in it. Cross these and continue along the other side of the hedge to a gate and stile. Having crossed this stile, take path T4a straight on, soon passing between hedges in the grounds of Turville Grange, to reach a gate leading out onto Turville Heath. Here bear half right to the end of a macadam road by the gates of Turville Grange, then turn left onto this road for your starting point.

WALK 8:   Cookley Green

Length of Walk: 7.8 miles / 12.6 Km
Starting Point: Bus shelter on Cookley Green.
Grid Ref: SU696902
Maps: OS Landranger Sheet 175
            OS Explorer Sheet 171 (or old Sheet 3)
            OS Pathfinder Sheets 1137 (SU69/79) & 1156 (SU68/78)
            Chiltern Society FP Maps Nos. 9 & 10
How to get there / Parking: Cookley Green, 6 miles
   northwest of Henley-on-Thames, may be reached from
   the town by taking the A4130 towards Oxford for 4.6 miles
   to Nettlebed, then turning right onto the B481 towards
   Watlington. After just over 2 miles, you round a sharp
   right-hand bend to emerge on Cookley Green, where, in a
   further 50 yards, there is a small car park on the right
   behind the village bus shelter.
Notes: In summer, heavy nettle growth may be encountered
   particularly on W11 and SW30.

Cookley Green, with its large triangular green at the point
where a number of ancient lanes meet, is today a picturesque
village with a spacious feel which has suffered little from
modern development. Like many villages with a green as their
focal point, Cookley Green is not an ancient parish and has no
church of its own, but grew up as a settlement to house the
farmworkers and servants of nearby Swyncombe Park, where
the manor house, church, rectory and a farm are situated.
   The walk, which combines spectacular escarpment downland with remote Chiltern beechwoods and is particularly
attractive in bluebell time (late-April to mid-May), first follows
the footsteps of generations of estate workers to Swyncombe,
before turning north over a wooded part of Swyncombe Down
to reach the Upper Icknield Way along the foot of the
escarpment. The return route then takes you by way of a
beautiful combe on the south side of Watlington Hill, before
climbing through beechwoods to Greenfield and continuing
through further woods to the airy hilltop common of Russell's
Water and an ancient green lane back to Cookley Green.

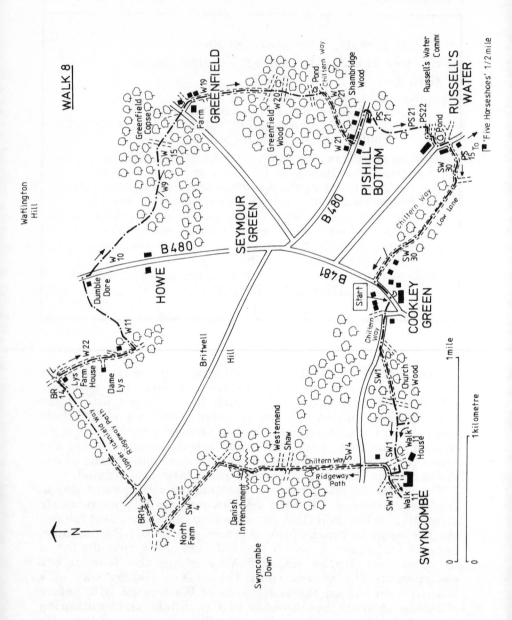

WALK 8

Wattington Hill

GREENFIELD
Greenfield Copse
Greenfield Farm W19
W9 15
W20
Greenfield Wood
Chiltern way
Pond
W21
Shambridge Wood
W21
W21
PS 21
PS21
PS22
To
PS 15
"Five Horseshoes" 1/2 mile
Russell's Water Commn
RUSSELL'S WATER
Pond
SW 30
PISHILL BOTTOM
SEYMOUR GREEN
B480
B481
Chiltern way
Low Lane
SW 30
Chiltern Way
COOKLEY GREEN
Start
W 10
Dumble Dore
B480
HOWE
W11
W 22
Lys Farm House
Dame Lys
BR 14
Upper Ichnield Way
Ridgeway Path
Britwell Hill
SW1
Church Wood
SW1
Walk 11
Church House
Westernend Shaw
Chiltern Way
SW 4
Ridgeway Path
SW13
Walk 11
SW 4
BR14
North Farm
SW 4
Danish Intrenchment
SWYNCOMBE
Swyncombe Down

←N—

1 mile
1 kilometre
0
0

44

Starting from Cookley Green's village bus shelter, cross the B481 and bear half left across the green to a road junction by a sycamore tree at the left-hand end of a row of Scots pines. Here bear slightly left onto the centre option of the three roads, joining the Chiltern Way and follow it until you reach a stile on the left about 50 yards into Church Wood. Fork half left over this stile onto path SW1 and follow its straight course, ignoring crossing tracks, to a kissing-gate on the far side of the wood, where you join the route of Walk 11. Go through this kissing-gate to enter Swyncombe Park with Swyncombe House, an Elizabethan manor house extensively rebuilt in the last century, coming into view ahead. Now bear slightly right, following a slight depression in the ground across the park to another kissing-gate at the corner of a fence under some yew trees. Go through this and follow a right-hand fence to a drive. Cross the drive and go straight on through the trees, then turn right through a gate into the churchyard of the eleventh-century St. Botolph's Church.

Pass left of the church to a small gate onto a rough road. Turn right onto this, leaving Walk 11 and joining the Ridgeway Path and follow it, bearing left to the top of a rise. Here cross a road and go through a kissing-gate by a field gate onto path SW4, which follows a track beside a left-hand hedge downhill, then the outside edge of a wood uphill to enter the wood. In the wood, ignore a crossing track and branching tracks and continue straight on uphill. At the top of this hill, Swyncombe Down, views open out through the trees across the Oxfordshire Plain towards Oxford. The track then descends again to cross a gully, part of an ancient earthwork known as the Danish Entrenchment. Now, leaving the Chiltern Way, ignore a branching path to the left and continue downhill. After emerging from the trees and bushes, the path turns left along a belt of trees towards North Farm, with views towards Britwell House on the next rise.

At the far end of the farm buildings at North Farm, turn right through a gap in the trees to the Upper Icknield Way, and ancient Celtic road named after the Iceni, the people of Boadicea. Turn right onto this wide hedged green road (BR14) and follow it for nearly a mile, crossing the Britwell Hill road. Where the Way narrows and divides into a cart-track and parallel footpath, continue through a belt of scrub until you reach a large house on the right. Join its drive and follow it straight on, then, after a few yards, leaving the Ridgeway, take the first of two right-hand turnings, a rough macadam drive and bridleway W22. Follow this for nearly half a mile passing Dame Lys (formerly Dame Alice Farm, named after Alice Chaucer, grand-daughter of the poet and Lady of Ewelme Manor in the fifteenth century), where the lane becomes unsurfaced. After passing a barn and cottage on the left, you then enter a belt of trees and turn left into another green lane (path W11) which soon becomes a narrow winding path between hedges and fences. Follow this until you reach the B480 road by a cottage called Dumble Dore, where a view opens out of Watlington Hill and One Tree Hill ahead.

Turn right onto the road and at the far end of the cottage fence, cross the road and take path W10 over a stile by a gate into a field, following a right-hand hedge straight on for a third of a mile to a stile into a belt of trees, where a winding path leads you over a rise and into a dip. Here cross a stile and take bridleway W9 straight on through a bridlegate then uphill. Disregard a path to the left to a stile into a field, then, at a waymarked fork, go left and follow waymarked path W15 uphill through a wood called Greenfield Copse, ignoring crossing tracks, until you reach a door onto a road at Greenfield.

Cross the road here and take bridleway W19 virtually straight on along a lane left of a green barn and past some cottages. Where the concrete surface turns right towards Shambridge House, leave it and continue straight on into a field. Now bear half right and follow a grassy track heading for a protruding finger of Greenfield Wood ahead. On reaching the woodland, follow a track straight on into it, winding downhill into the valley bottom. Here ignore a crossing track and take bridleway W20, a winding waymarked path, straight on over the next rise into a further dip, disregarding three crossing tracks at the top of the rise. In the dip ignore a further crossing track and go straight on past a pond to your left to a waymarked T-junction. Here turn right onto bridleway W21, rejoining the Chiltern Way. After some 350 yards, this waymarked track turns left and descends to emerge from the wood into a farmyard. From here metal gates lead out onto the B480 road in Pishill Bottom. (Although pronounced 'Pis-hill' with a short 'i', the name is actually a corruption of 'Peas-hill'.)

Turn left along the road and follow it for about 350 yards past some cottages until you reach a gravel drive on your right leading to Glade House. Turn right onto this drive (path PS21) and where the drive turns rights, take a sunken woodland path straight on uphill. Eventually this winding path levels out and leads you onto Russell's Water Common. Follow the right-hand edge of the common until you reach a green lane (bridleway PS22) leading off it. Turn right into this lane and follow it into Russell's Water.

Russell's Water, which is named after a local brickmaker and his pond in the centre of the village, is a scattered community ranged along the edge of its extensive hilltop common on the ancient parish boundary between Pishill and Swyncombe. Its origins are obscure, but it is known to have existed since at least the late seventeenth century and it may occupy the site of a settlement known as Pishill Venables which was recorded in the thirteenth century.

At a T-junction of tracks, turn right onto a track past the picturesque village pond, then turn left onto a macadam road. On reaching a small green on the left, turn right by the entrance to Tithe Barn into a rough lane (bridleway PS15, soon becoming SW30) and follow it past a white house with shutters, descending slowly at first. At a gate directly ahead, turn sharp right and follow the lane steeply downhill to the bottom of the valley. On reaching a T-junction with another lane, turn right (still on SW30) and ignoring turnings and gates to right and left, follow this lane, Law Lane, through a belt of trees and a copse, then past a few houses to the B481 at the edge of Cookley Green. Here turn left and follow its left-hand verge back to your point of departure.

WALK 9:   Maidensgrove

Length of Walk: (A)   5.9 miles / 9.4 Km
                                (B)   3.4 miles / 5.4 Km

Starting Point: Bend in road on Russell's Water Common, near Maidensgrove.

Grid Ref: SU718887

Maps: OS Landranger Sheet 175
OS Explorer Sheet 171 (or old Sheet 3)
OS Pathfinder Sheet 1156 (SU68/78)
Chiltern Society FP Maps Nos. 2 & 9

How to get there / Parking: Maidensgrove, 4.5 miles north-west of Henley-on-Thames, may be reached from the town by taking the A4130 towards Oxford for 1.5 miles. At the far end of a long straight known as The Fairmile, turn right onto the Assendons and Stonor road. At Stonor, turn left into a concealed turn signposted to Maidensgrove and Russell's Water. After nearly a mile, ignore a turning to the left signposted Maidensgrove and continue straight on for a quarter mile out onto Russell's Water Common. Park on the verge at a sharp right-hand bend where the road joins the southern hedge of the common and a rough lane leads off the common. Cars may be parked within 15 feet of the road or this lane, but should not obstruct either.

Maidensgrove, referred to in several late mediaeval documents as 'Menygrove' (meaning a 'common clearing'), is the collective name for two small hamlets about three-quarters of a mile apart, Maidensgrove and Upper Maidensgrove, which are separated by part of the wide expanse of Russell's Water Common. Maidensgrove is the larger with two farms and a number of cottages as well as several modern properties, while Upper Maidensgrove boasts a farm and a pub. Both the hamlets and the common are situated on a high ridge which affords extensive views over the hilltops and deep valleys.

Both alternative walks descend into the upper part of Bix Bottom and the ancient road to Oxford and return from Park Corner at the head of the valley by way of Upper Maidensgrove. Walk A additionally climbs to Nettlebed Common and Nettlebed, returning on a parallel route.

Both walks start from the bend in the road near Maidensgrove on Russell's Water Common and head southwards along SW31, a rough lane called Hatch Lane and part of the Chiltern Way, leaving the common at this point. Where the right-hand hedge ends by an old gate, leave the lane and take path SW22, bearing half right across a field to a stile just left of a corner of Big Ashes Plantation ahead. This woodland in Bix Bottom is part of the Warburg Nature Reserve owned by the Berkshire, Buckinghamshire and Oxfordshire Naturalists Trust and is noted for its rare chalkland plants. On entering the wood, follow a path straight on along its top edge. Where the edge of the wood drops down to the left, cross a stile and leave the wood. Here bear half left across a field to a stile into a protruding finger of woodland. Cross this and drop steeply through the wood and over another stile, then bear half right across a field to a gate and stile leading to a junction of lanes in Bix Bottom, the major one of which is part of the ancient Henley to Oxford road.

Here **Walk B** leaves the Chiltern Way and goes straight on along the lane (SW28) and follows it for one mile, soon passing a wood and Westwood Manor Farm to the left and later passing the appropriately named Dark Wood to the left. At a fork just after this, go right. (Now disregard the next three paragraphs.)

Walk A also leaves the Chiltern Way and goes straight on along the lane (SW28), but just before the start of a wood to the left, it turns left over a stile onto path SW21 and follows the outside edge of the wood to a crossing track coming out of the wood. Bear half right across this track to cross another stile, then take an obvious woodland path straight on for a third of a mile to reach a stile at the far end of the wood leading into a field. Cross this and bear slightly left to join a left-hand hedge at a corner of it and follow it straight on to a stile. Having crossed this, follow the left-hand hedge past a pond, then continue between hedges to reach a drive at Magpies on the edge of Nettlebed's wooded common. Turn left onto this drive (bridleway NE16) and after about 150 yards, at a sharp right-hand bend, leave the drive and go straight on along a woodland path (still NE16). Where another path crosses diagonally, turn half left onto it and follow it until you reach a major crossing path. Cross this, bearing half right and follow a waymarked path, ignoring several branching paths to the right, until you emerge at the top of Windmill Hill by a telegraph pole and underground reservoir. Now bear half right down a lane to the B481 road at Nettlebed.

Turn left onto the B481 and follow it to the A4130. Here it is well worthwhile to take a slight detour turning left and left again to visit the old brick kiln. This has been restored in recent years and serves as a monument to the local brick industry which dates back to at least the fifteenth century and which was responsible for digging all the old clay- and sandpits you will have noticed on Windmill Hill. Otherwise, cross the A4130 and turn right along its pavement. Here the old coaching inns and cottages and early Victorian parish church provide examples of the local brick. On leaving the village, follow the A4130 straight on for a further 300 yards. At the far end of a left-hand bend, cross the A4130 carefully and take path NE4, a sunken lane between hedges. On reaching a barbed-wire fence ahead, turn right over a stile and follow the outside edge of a copse uphill to a corner of the field. Here turn left over a stile by a gate and bear slightly right across a field to a stile just left of the near corner of Groveridge Wood. Cross this and follow waymarked path NU16 straight on through the wood for 170 yards until you reach a crossing track (path NU30). Turn right onto this track and follow it for a quarter mile to a wide crossing track known as Bushes Lane. Here take waymarked path NE20 straight on through Copse Wood, disregarding a crossing path at one point and after a quarter mile reaching the B481.

Turn left along its verge and at a left-hand bend, turn right onto path NE6 into woodland on Nettlebed Common. Inside the woods, you soon bear right, then, at a fork, go left and follow an obvious path for over a quarter mile, looking out for a branching path to your left leading to a stile into a field. Turn left onto this path (NE29), crossing the stile where a fine view opens out ahead across Bix Bottom towards Russell's Water and Maidensgrove, then bear left across the field (now on path SW38), heading towards Darkwood Farm, to a stile left of a hedge junction in the bottom. Cross this stile and follow a right-hand hedge and later a copse uphill. Where the fence of the copse bears right, go straight on towards a cottage to cross a stile, then bear slightly left across the next field to a stile by a gate left of the cottage. Having crossed this and a further stile, follow a right-hand fence to a stile by the corner of Dark Wood. Cross this and go straight on along the edge of the wood to a lane (SW28). Turn left onto this, then almost immediately fork right.

Now **Walks A and B** turn right onto a road at Park Corner and follow it to a sharp left-hand bend. Here, rejoining the Chiltern Way, turn right onto hedged bridleway SW15 and follow it to a gate at the far end of this green lane. Here do not go through the gate, but turn right over a stile onto path SW29 and follow a left-hand hedge straight on through two fields. Where the hedge turns left in the second field, go straight on across the field to a concealed gate at the right-hand corner of a copse ahead. Go through this gate and follow the outside edge of the copse, soon turning left, then, in a corner of the field, turn right and follow the left-hand hedge to cross two stiles in the next corner. Now bear slightly left, passing just right of a clump of trees

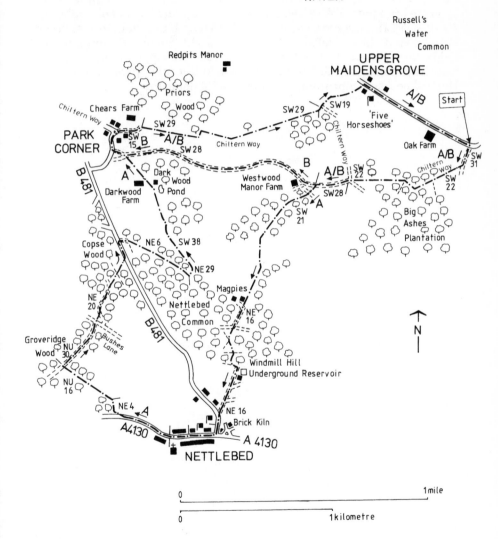

RUSSELL'S
WATER

Russell's
Water
Common

Redpits Manor

UPPER
MAIDENSGROVE

A/B

Start

Priors
Wood

Chiltern Way

Chears Farm

SW 29

SW29

SW19

'Five
Horseshoes'

PARK
CORNER

SW 29

A/B

SW
15

B

Chiltern Way

Chiltern Way

Oak Farm

A/B

SW
31

SW 28

B 481

A

Dark
Wood
Pond

Westwood
Manor Farm

B

A/B

SW
22

Chiltern Way

SW
22

Darkwood
Farm

SW28

A

Big
Ashes
Plantation

Copse
Wood

NE 6

SW 38

SW
21

NE 29

NE
20

Magpies

B 481

Nettlebed
Common

NE
16

Groveridge
Wood

NU
30

Bushes
Lane

NU
16

N

NE 4

A

Windmill Hill

Underground Reservoir

A4130

NE 16

Brick Kiln

A 4130

NETTLEBED

0   1mile

0   1kilometre

51

concealing an old pit and continuing straight on to join a left-hand hedge in the valley bottom where a sporadic line of trees marking an old hedgeline joins it. From here, follow the left-hand hedge to reach two stiles into the corner of a wood, then follow the left-hand hedge through the wood to a stile leading onto a bridleway. Leaving the Chiltern Way again, cross this stile, the bridleway and another stile opposite onto path SW19 and follow a left-hand hedge steeply uphill to a rail-stile. Having crossed this, climb a steep bank and cross another stile, then follow a left-hand hedge straight on uphill through two fields to a gate and stile leading to a road at Upper Maidensgrove. Here turn right and follow the road for half a mile, passing the 'Five Horseshoes' and continuing to your point of departure.

WALK 10: Nuffield

Length of Walk: (A) 8.1 miles / 13.1 Km
 (B) 4.5 miles / 7.2 Km

Starting Point: Nuffield Church.

Grid Ref: SU668874

Maps: OS Landranger Sheet 175
 OS Explorer Sheet 171 (or old Sheet 3)
 OS Pathfinder Sheet 1156 (SU68/78)
 Chiltern Society FP Map No. 15

How to get there / Parking: Nuffield, 6.5 miles northwest of Henley-on-Thames, may be reached from the town by taking the A4130 towards Oxford for 6 miles, then turning left onto a road signposted to Nuffield, Stoke Row and Checkendon. After just over half a mile, turn right onto a road signposted to Nuffield Church to reach the church on the left after some 300 yards. Cars can be parked on wide grass verges east of the church.

Nuffield, with its extensive heathy common most of which is used as a golf course, is today best known for its associations with the car-maker, William Morris, later Lord Nuffield, who lived at Nuffield Place and took the name of the village not only for his title, but also for his charitable foundations such as Nuffield College, Oxford. Although the Domesday Book suggests that Nuffield was only an insignificant detached portion of Chalgrove parish, 6 miles to the north on the Oxfordshire plain, the construction of its church in the twelfth century suggests that the hilltop village had, by then, become a separate parish. This church, indeed, boasts a Norman font with a Latin inscription and an early brass dated 1360 depicting Beneit Engliss, after whom English Farm, which you pass during the walk, is thought to be named.

 Both alternative walks explore the quiet upland plateau to the east and south of Nuffield with its variety of farmland and woodland and while both walks also skirt the top of the Chiltern escarpment with long-range views across the Thames Valley, Walk A additionally descends the escarpment to Hailey and Woodhouse Farm with particularly fine views of the Thames Valley and Berkshire Downs and Sinodun Hills beyond.

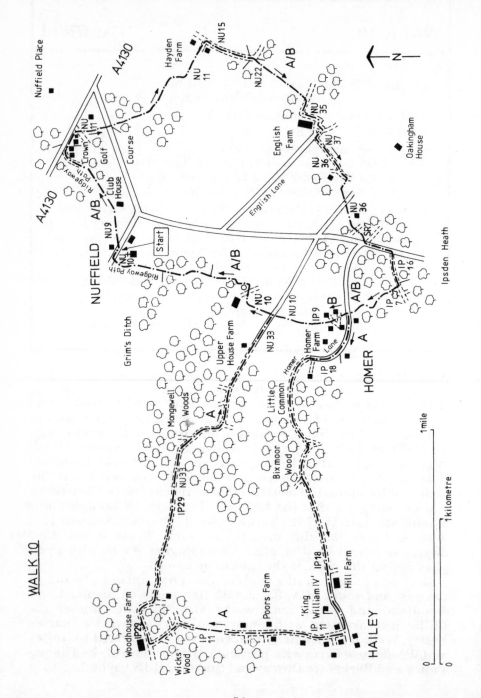

WALK 10

54

Starting from Nuffield Church, **both walks** take the Ridgeway Path (NU9) over a stile opposite the eastern end of the churchyard and bear half right across a field to a waymarked gap left of the golf clubhouse. Now follow a path marked by a series of seven white posts straight on across the golf course, watching out for driving golfers. Eventually you pass between a cottage and an outbuilding and follow the cottage drive to the A4130 near the 'Crown'. Go past the 'Crown', then take path NU11, keeping right of an 'island' of grass and going straight on across the golf course, passing left of a large bunker. Now bear slightly right and head for a gap in the trees leading to another road. Cross this and take path NU11 straight on to a gap in the next tree belt, then bear slightly right to another gap and go straight on to a third. By the thirteenth tee, bear half right to a stile in the left-hand hedge near the corner of a wood. Leaving the golf course, cross this stile and follow the left-hand hedge to a stile in it. Cross this and follow the other side of the hedge to cross another stile. Now follow a right-hand fence and sporadic hedge to a field corner, where you turn right and follow a right-hand hedge to Hayden Farm, where you go straight on between farm buildings.

Beyond the buildings, at the end of a concrete road, turn right onto bridleway NU15, a stony lane. Where it turns left into a belt of trees, take path NU22 straight on over a stile into the right-hand of two fields. Now bear half right across the field, heading for a stile at the left-hand end of a group of trees in front of English Farm. Here turn right into a stony lane (path NU35) and follow it, swinging left of the farm. Where it enters a farmyard, turn left over a stile and then right into English Lane (NU37).

Where the lane becomes macadamed, turn left into a stony lane leading to a stile and New Zealand (barbed-wire) gate, where the large modern neo-Georgian Oakingham House can be seen to your left. Here take path NU36, following a grassy track beside a right-hand fence to cross a cattle grid near a large house. Now join a drive, swinging right then left between two ponds. Just beyond a pair of oak trees, turn right to follow the rear side of a beech hedge past a tennis court to a stile, then bear left across a field to a stile into a lane. Cross this and another stile opposite and bear slightly right across a field to a telegraph pole at the corner of a fence. Here bear half left beside a left-hand fence to a stile into woodland at Ipsden Heath. Take path SR7 straight on through the wood, crossing a track and eventually emerging onto a road at Homer Turn. Turn left along the major road, soon turning right into the stony Urquhart Lane (IP16). After 300 yards turn right onto crossing path IP7 passing through a plantation, then along the inside edge of the wood to a stile. Cross this and follow a winding sunken way uphill to a stile and gates into a lane at Homer.

Here **Walk B** takes path IP9 straight on along a gated drive. Where the drive bears left, keep straight on, passing left of the farmhouse and a ring of staddle stones to cross a stile by an old gate. Here go straight on along the edge of a wood at first then continuing across a field to cross a stile left of a powerline. Now take path NU10 straight on across the next field to a hedge gap leading to a road. Cross this and follow a left-hand hedge straight on, rejoining Walk A. Now omit the next paragraph.

Walk A turns left into Homer Lane and follows it for 1.4 miles, ignoring all branching tracks. Where the drive to 'Fludger's Wood' branches left, the surface of the lane (now IP18) changes from macadam to flint. After passing through Little Common and Bixmoor Wood, at a fork keep left with the Berkshire Downs and Thames Valley coming into view as you descend the escarpment. On nearing Hailey, the surface reverts to macadam, then having passed the 'King William IV' with its interesting collection of antique farm implements, turn right onto path IP11, a macadam road opposite the drive to the first left-hand bungalow, and follow this for a third of a mile, soon losing its macadam surface. At Poors Farm, disregard a branch to the left and take a fenced track straight on, ignoring a further left-hand branch. Where the track enters a field and peters out, go straight on across the field to a stile by a cattle grid into Wicks Wood. Now take a woodland track straight on, ignoring all branching or crossing tracks, to reach a rough road (IP29) at Woodhouse Farm. Turn right onto this following the edge of the wood. Where the road forks, fork left away from the wood and follow a track uphill, where there are soon fine views behind. After half a mile the track enters Mongewell Woods (becoming NU33), where you ignore all branching tracks. After leaving the woods, you pass Upper House Farm, then, on reaching a crossing powerline, turn left onto path NU10 following a left-hand hedge.

Where the left-hand hedge and fence end, **both walks** bear slightly right heading for the timber-framed Ridgeway Farmhouse ahead to reach a post-and-rail fence. Here turn right and follow this fence to a stile. Cross this and a drive and take a fenced path to a corner, then turn left onto a path between a hedge and a fence past a pond to enter a belt of trees. Now follow the path past a pit, then cross a ladder-stile and follow a right-hand hedge straight on to enter a belt of trees. Continue straight on through the trees to a stile onto the Ridgeway Path. Crossing Grim's Ditch, an ancient earthwork of uncertain origin, follow the path straight on to a kissing-gate. Now follow a right-hand belt of trees to reach a road at Nuffield, where you turn right for your starting point.

WALK 11:   Ewelme

Length of Walk: (A) 7.5 miles / 12.0 Km
                    (B) 3.0 miles / 4.9 Km

Starting Point: Recreation ground car park, Ewelme.

Grid Ref: SU648912

Maps: OS Landranger Sheet 175 (or 164 – B only)
OS Explorer Sheet 171 (or old Sheet 3)
OS Pathfinder Sheets 1137 (SU 69/79) (A+B)
& 1156 (SU68/78) (A only)
Chiltern Society FP Map No. 10

How to get there / Parking: Ewelme, 2.7 miles northeast
of Wallingford, may be reached from the roundabout at
the northern junction of the A4074 and A4130 at
Crowmarsh Gifford by taking a road signposted to
Ewelme for 1.5 miles to a T-junction. Here turn right,
then immediately left and left again descending into
Ewelme. At a sharp left-hand bend in the village, turn
right onto a road signposted to Swyncombe and Cookley
Green and after about 350 yards the car park is on the
right.

Ewelme, today, is an idyllic sleepy Oxfordshire village with its
cottages and old watercress beds nestling in the folds of the
foothills of the southern Chiltern escarpment. The village
became prominent in the early fifteenth century, when the
poet Chaucer's son married the heiress to the manor. This
prominence was furthered by their daughter's marriage into
the ill-fated Suffolk family. On the Suffolks' downfall, the
manor passed into the hands of the Crown resulting in the
construction of Ewelme Palace by Henry VII. During the
course of the sixteenth century, the palace was used by Henry
VIII, whose bathing activities led to the pool at the head of the
stream (more recently a watercress bed) being named King's
Pool. The palace also served as a childhood home to Princess
Elizabeth, later Elizabeth I. After this period, however, the
manor was sold and the palace allowed to decay.

Both walks are of high scenic value, Walk A, ascending the
escarpment and including the ancient hamlet of Swyncombe,
the name of which means 'valley of the wild boar'.

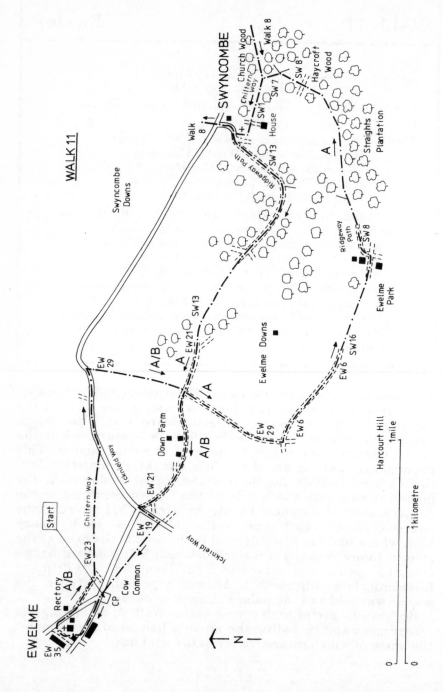

WALK 11

Starting from the car park by the village recreation ground, both walks take the lower road into the village until you reach the primary school. This was built in 1437 by William and Alice, Duke and Duchess of Suffolk, as a grammar school and is now the oldest primary school building in England. Just past the school, turn half right across a green to join a macadam lane (path EW35) passing the almshouses and church, also built by William and Alice around 1437. These are both worth visiting. The almshouses were built around a quadrangle in brick and timber (including some unusual herring-bone pattern brickwork) in a fashion reminiscent of Oxford colleges. The church contains a magnificent fifteenth-century carved oak font cover, an alabaster effigy of the founder's wife, Alice Chaucer and her parents' tomb with brasses depicting the poet's son and his wife, while Jerome K. Jerome, author of 'Three Men in a Boat', lies buried in the churchyard.

At the top of this lane, turn right onto a road and just past the rectory on the left, joining the Chiltern Way, fork left onto path EW23 up a rough track which soon gives a view of Ewelme Down and Ewelme Down House straight ahead. Follow this track, disregarding a garden gate to your left, to enter a field where a view of Swyncombe Down opens up ahead. Now continue straight on, crossing another stile, then bear slightly left to a third stile. Be sure to stop and look around you at this spot, where there are good views at all compass points including, directly behind you, Wittenham Clumps, in ancient times a lookout over the Thames opposite Dorchester.

From here, head for the top corner of an apparently triangular field on the side of Swyncombe Down, soon dropping down to a gate and stile onto the Icknield Way road, an ancient Celtic road named after the Iceni, in Warren Bottom. Continue straight on along this road over a small rise. Having left the Chiltern Way, at a left-hand bend, turn right through a gap beside double gates and follow bridleway EW29 beside a left-hand hedge. After more than a quarter mile, the bridleway leaves this hedge, joining a right-hand hedge and following it until you reach a macadam drive. Here, if wishing to do **Walk B**, turn right onto this drive (bridleway EW21) and then read the last paragraph for the continuation.

Walk A continues straight on across the drive onto a rough farm road (still EW29). Follow this for half a mile to a crossways at the foot of Harcourt Hill ahead. Here turn left onto bridleway EW6, a grassy track up the valley floor, heading towards Ewelme Park House which can be seen on the skyline at the head of the valley. After nearly half a mile the track briefly becomes enclosed between a hedge and a fence. Now take bridleway SW16, following a right-hand hedge straight on uphill. Near the top of the hill, go through a hedge gap into a lane which soon gives a close view of the Ewelme Park House to the right, while to the left an attractive pond is hidden in the bushes.

At the far end of the garden wall, turn left between farm buildings onto the Ridgeway Path (SW8). At the far end of the farmyard, turn right along a lane until it opens into a field. Now continue straight on following a right-hand hedge until it turns left. Here leave the Ridgeway Path, forking right through a hedge gap to cross a stile into Swyncombe Park, then take path SW8 following the right-hand fence through several large clumps of trees. Through the trees to the left, Swyncombe House, an Elizabethan manor house extensively rebuilt in the nineteenth century, and the hamlet including the largely Saxon church of St. Botolph may be glimpsed in places backed by Swyncombe Down.

After half a mile, at the far end of this parkland field, cross a stile to enter Haycroft Wood, then bear half left, soon crossing a macadam drive and eventually reaching a wide fire-break. At the far side of this fire-break, turn left onto path SW7, following the inside edge of storm-ravaged woodland downhill to reach a crossing path. Here turn left through a kissing-gate onto path SW1 (temporarily joining Walk 8 and the Chiltern Way) and follow a depression in the ground across Swyncombe Park to a kissing-gate under some yew trees. Now follow the waymarked path through the trees and across a drive, then, on reaching the churchyard of St. Botolph's, turn right through a gate into it and follow the path past the church.

At the far side of the churchyard turn left, leaving Walk 8 and the Chiltern Way and rejoining the Ridgeway Path. Now bear slightly left through gates into the tree-lined ancient road to Ewelme (now bridleway SW13). Follow this down the valley for two-thirds of a mile, disregarding the Ridgeway Path branching left, until reaching a crossways. Here go straight on, then, at a fork, keep left. On leaving the wood, follow a right-hand hedge straight on until you enter another wood. Now follow bridleway EW21 through the trees to join a macadam drive which shortly crosses the outward route of the walk.

Walks A and B now follow this drive straight on for two-thirds of a mile, passing Ewelme Down Farm. Where the drive forks, bear right soon reaching gates leading to the Icknield Way. Turn left onto this road, passing the other entrance to the drive, then, opposite a green lane, turn right onto path EW19 through a kissing-gate onto Cow Common and head slightly right of some distant buildings, gradually crossing the valley bottom to a kissing-gate by the car park.

WALK 12: Crowmarsh Gifford

Length of Walk: 9.1 miles / 14.6 Km or 9.4 miles / 15.1 Km

Starting Point: Entrance to Riverside Park car park at eastern end of Wallingford Bridge.

Grid Ref: SU612894

Maps: OS Landranger Sheet 175
OS Explorer Sheet 171 (or old Sheet 3)
OS Pathfinder Sheet 1156 (SU68/78)
Chiltern Society FP Map No. 15

Parking: A public car park is signposted on the north side of the road at the eastern (Crowmarsh) end of Wallingford Bridge.

The twin villages of Crowmarsh Gifford and Newnham Murren, which face each other on either side of the road to Wallingford Bridge (formerly their parish boundary), are today barely more than a pleasant suburb of the town. Before 1974, however, they were in a different county from Wallingford, which used to be in Berkshire, and going further back still, it would seem from the location of Newnham Murren Church in the fields half a mile south of the main road that the villages were once completely separate entities and it was only the economic influence and convenience of the former main road with the river bridge which caused the bulk of Newnham Murren's population to move to live on the parish boundary. Be that as it may, despite the county boundary and the physical barrier of the river, Wallingford and the twin villages on the old Oxfordshire bank shared a common history, as the present graceful bridge built in 1809 stands on the foundations of a mediaeval structure which was, in turn, built to replace the nearby ford which gave the town its name. This is one of the places where the conquering Norman armies are believed to have crossed the Thames in 1066 and its strategic importance can be seen from the Norman castle built in Wallingford, which was subsequently destroyed in a Civil War siege in 1646, and the fact that the town is believed to be the first to have been granted a royal charter in 1155.

The walk takes you from this historic river crossing through the unusually open rolling Chiltern foothills to the south-east

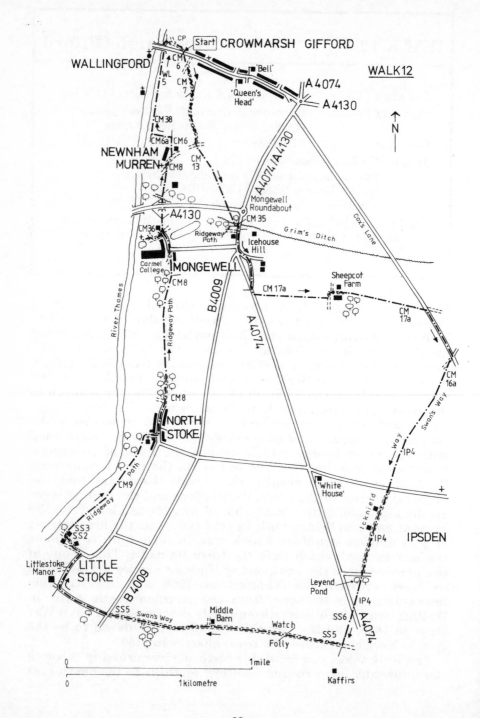

CROWMARSH GIFFORD

WALK 12

with extensive views of the Thames valley and surrounding hills at a number of points before dropping down to the river at Little Stoke and leading you back through a series of interesting and attractive riverside settlements to culminate with the beautiful section of towpath approaching Wallingford Bridge.

Starting from the entrance to the Riverside Park car park at the Crowmarsh end of Wallingford Bridge, cross the road and go through a gap at the end of the bridge parapet onto path CM6. Now bear half left across a field to a gap in a corner of the field. Here cross a track and bear right onto the hedged bridleway CM7 known as Watery Lane. Follow this for nearly half a mile and where its hedges end, continue between fences until you reach a concrete road. Turn right onto this, then immediately left through a fence gap onto path CM13, bearing half left across a field to a hedge gap left of an elder bush. Now bear half right across the next field heading just right of a cluster of lampposts at Mongewell Roundabout to cross a stile then climb a steep bank to the A4130 Wallingford Bypass. Cross this road and a footbridge opposite, then bear half left through a plantation. Now go through a hedge gap and turn left onto the Ridgeway Path (CM35), soon crossing a stile to reach the A4074.

Cross this road and turn right along its verge ignoring the Ridgeway Path to your left. At the Icehouse Hill junction with the B4009, turn left onto a side road. Where this road forks, bear right and continue along it until you rejoin the A4074. Now follow its left-hand verge for some 60 yards with fine views to your right across the Thames Valley to the Berkshire Downs beyond, then turn left through a gate onto bridleway CM17a, following a left-hand fence over a slight rise for over a third of a mile with fine views of the Chiltern escarpment opening out ahead. On reaching Sheepcot Farm, turn left onto a concrete road, soon turning right. Where the road forks, go straight on between barns, then, just past a silo, keep left of a hedge to enter a field and follow this hedge straight on. Where the hedge turns right, leave it and go straight on across the field to a hedge gap and in the next field, continue straight on, heading for black barns at the distant Woodhouse Farm, to reach a gate into Cox's Lane. Turn right onto this road and follow it for a quarter mile to a road junction. Here turn right onto bridleway CM16a, a fenced track which is also part of the ancient Icknield Way and the modern Swan's Way long-distance bridleway. Where this track enters a field, fork left off it, keeping left of a fence and following the obvious bridleway (later IP4) straight on for three quarters of a mile. Ipsden Church, which soon comes into view in trees on a low hilltop to your left, was built in about 1200 as a chapel-of-ease for the parish of North Stoke, but following the reversal of the respective size and importance of the two villages, it later became the parish church.

On reaching the road leading to the church, cross it and take a fenced track (still IP4) straight on. By a bungalow, the track narrows and continues between hedges to another road. Cross this and go straight on into a copse concealing Leyend Pond. By a chestnut tree at the far side of the copse, look out for a monument in bushes to your right which has a strange story. Erected by Edward Reade, a brother of the Victorian novelist Charles Reade, in 1860, the monument marks the spot where their mother had, in 1827, had a vision of their eldest brother, John Thurlow Reade who was then in India, coming towards her in distress. She took this to mean that he had died and not received a Christian burial and some time later news indeed arrived that John had died and been buried in the Indian jungle. It is said that the monument was therefore erected to lay his ghost.

On leaving the copse, go straight on to a hedge gap at the top of a rise. Go through this bear half left across the A4074 to a fence gap leading to bridleway SS6. Having passed through this, go straight on over a rise, heading for the right-hand end of woodland on the skyline. On reaching a crossing grass track (bridleway SS5), turn right onto it and follow it for 1.3 miles over a hill called Watch Folly and past Middle Barn and a copse to reach the B4009 at a road junction. The name Watch Folly arises from this hill with its superb panoramic views having been used as a look-out post to give early warning of the highwaymen who used to frequent the locality and legend has it that a boy sent to perform this task was once hanged by highwaymen from the single tree which used to cap its summit.

Cross the B4009 and take a minor road straight on towards the hamlet of Little Stoke. At a sharp bend by Littlestoke Manor, a mainly Georgian house of Tudor origin, follow the road round to the right and then ignore a branching drive to your left. On reaching a T-junction, turn left into a cul-de-sac road and by a thatched barn, fork right through a white gate onto path SS2, the gravel drive to Little Stoke House and Ferry Cottage. At a turning circle, keep straight on passing left of a cottage with an unusual evergreen magnolia. Just past the cottage turn right onto fenced path SS3 (the Ridgeway Path) which leads you to a stile. Having crossed this, follow a left-hand hedge, later a fence, straight on parallel to the River Thames to your left to reach a footbridge and stile. Cross these and go straight on across a field to a further stile, then take path CM9 following a left-hand fence to a stile into scrubby marshland. Here go straight on along a fenced path skirting the marshland to a stile into a riverside garden. Cross the stile and the garden to reach a fence gap, then bear half right to reach a stile into North Stoke churchyard. Now follow a path passing left of this thirteenth-century church, which is of interest for its thirteenth-century murals and fourteenth-century sundial, then bearing right to join a macadam path leading to a lychgate into Church Lane.

At a T-junction turn left along the picturesque village street passing an old watermill. Where its macadam surface ends, take bridleway CM8 straight on along a wide tree-lined avenue. On emerging onto a golf course, follow its left-hand hedge straight on and at its far end, go straight on through a fence gap into Mongewell Park. Here follow the edge of a copse straight on ignoring a branching path to the right, then continue along a gravel track and macadam drive past outbuildings of Carmel College to reach a bend in the road at Mongewell. Follow this road straight on, then at a junction, if wishing to visit Mongewell's ruined Norman church and see the attractive grounds and striking modern architecture of Carmel College, turn left onto the left-hand of two macadam drives (path CM36). Where this drive forks, turn right onto a drive signposted to Founders House, then, on nearing this house, fork left off the drive to a gate into the churchyard. This church was closed in 1932 and after the roof of its nave had collapsed, the chancel was walled off and restored in 1953. Now retrace your steps to the road junction.

From this junction, take the bollarded, paved bridleway CM8 northwards, soon leaving the Ridgeway Path and passing through a tunnel under the A4130 Wallingford Bypass. (If flooded, take the stone track to your left to cross the A4130 on the surface.) Now continue through a belt of trees concealing the ancient earthwork known as Grim's Ditch. Just beyond this, where the paved path turns right, leave it and follow the hedged path straight on. On joining a farm track, Newnham Murren's disused Norman church is to your left partially concealed by bushes. Follow this track until you reach a pair of cottages. Here fork left over a stile onto path CM6 and follow a right-hand fence past the cottages to a stile. Cross this stile and go straight on, then about 20 yards beyond a cattle trough, turn left onto undefined path CM6a going straight across the field to the bank of the River Thames. Here turn right onto the towpath (CM38, later WL5) and follow it for half a mile with fine views across the river of Wallingford including the Norman St. Leonard's Church and the eighteenth-century St. Peter's Church with its distinctive spire. On reaching Wallingford Bridge, pass underneath it and turn right for your point of departure.

WALK 13:   Woodcote

Length of Walk: (A) 7.2 miles / 11.5 Km
                      (B) 4.2 miles / 6.7 Km
Starting Point: Crossroads near Woodcote Village Hall.
Grid Ref: SU645821
Maps: OS Landranger Sheet 175
           OS Explorer Sheet 171 (or old Sheet 3)
           OS Pathfinder Sheet 1156 (SU68/78)
           Chiltern Society FP Maps (A) Nos. 15 & 16
                                     (B) No. 16 only
How to get there / Parking: Woodcote, 7 miles northwest
   of Reading, may be reached from the town by taking the
   A4155 towards Henley across the Thames to Caversham,
   then forking left onto the A4074 towards Wallingford.
   Follow this road for over 6 miles, then turn left for
   Woodcote, looking out after half a mile for a car park on
   the left beside the village hall about 100 yards short of a
   crossroads with the B471.
Notes: Various paths on both alternative walks are prone to
   heavy nettle growth in Summer.

At first sight, Woodcote with its profusion of modern and
Victorian red-brick houses gives the impression of being a
village of relatively modern origin, but a close examination of
its church reveals the fact that it was first built in Norman
times. The reason for this is that the village, the name of which
means 'cottage(s) in the woods', until it was enclosed in 1853,
consisted merely of a few cottages and farms scattered around
a large upland common similar to that still to be found at
Russell's Water and it is only since then that a considerable
expansion has occurred. It is also interesting to note that the
church was constructed as a chapel-of-ease for the riverside
parish of South Stoke and it was only in 1952 that Woodcote,
which had, by then, far outstripped its 'mother village' in size,
became a separate civil parish.

Both versions of the walk, indeed, explore some of the
extensive woodland which still surrounds the village as its
name suggests, but both, in particular Walk A, also emerge

from the woods in places to give superb views across the Thames Valley towards the Berkshire Downs, Sinodun Hills and, on a clear day, the Corallian Hills around Oxford.

Both **Walks A and B** start from the crossroads near Woodcote Village Hall and take the B471, Goring Road towards Goring and Whitchurch for a third of a mile to its junction with Beech Lane. Here turn right into Beech Lane, then, at a double road junction, turn left into Wood Lane. Where the road ends, take fenced path WD2 extending its right-hand pavement until you enter a wood called Fox Covert. In the wood, turn left onto path WD17, immediately forking right and following the path straight on through the wood to a gate and stile where you rejoin the B471. Turn right onto this road, following it downhill to a crossroads and up again to a left-hand bend. Here turn right over a stile by gates onto path GH22 and bear slightly left across a field to pass the left side of two clumps of trees concealing old chalkpits. At the far end of the second clump, bear slightly left across the field, heading just right of a telegraph pole in a fenced compound ahead, to reach a gate and stile into a green lane leading you between cottage gardens at Little Heath to a stony lane (bridleway GH13).

Turn right into this bridleway and follow it straight on, soon descending through Old Elvendon Wood with views of Elvendon Priory down the valley to your left to reach Battle Road. Turn left onto this road and at the top of a rise, fork right through a gate onto bridleway GO13, a woodland track which soon emerges into a field. Here ignore a gate ahead and bear slightly right following a fenced track along the top edge of the field. Where the track turns right through the hedge, follow it (now on path GO14) and continue over the hill, eventually passing between a barn and a belt of trees to reach a crossroads. Here turn right into Beech Lane. After nearly a quarter mile, soon after the commencement of Elmorepark Wood to your right, turn left onto path GH69, a stony track across a field into High Wood. Where you enter the wood, leave the track and take path WD29 straight on through the trees down a dip and up again to join a winding track. Now follow this along the inside edge of the wood bearing left at first. By a corner of the field to your right, ignore various tracks going deeper into the wood and bear right continuing to follow the inside edge of the wood until, at the far end of the wood, you emerge into a field near the attractive timber-framed Broad Street Farm. Now bear slightly left to reach a hedge gap leading to a road. Turn right onto this road and follow it past Broad Street Farm, then turn left through a former gateway onto path WD7 where a panoramic view opens out of the Thames Valley and Oxfordshire Plain beyond with Didcot Power Station and the maltings at Wallingford as prominent landmarks. Now follow the right-hand hedge downhill until you reach the corner of Dean Wood to your right. Here, if wishing to take **Walk A**, omit the next paragraph.

Walk B now continues downhill along the outside edge of Dean Wood, dropping into a sunken gully and ignoring the first path into the wood. On reaching a second, more prominent path into the wood (WD28), turn right onto it disregarding branching paths to left and right and entering a plantation. At the far side of the plantation, continue to follow the path bearing left and ignoring two branching paths to the right. By the corner of a field to your right, the path then swings right, generally following the contours of the hill. After a further 150 yards, disregard a branching path to the left and take path WD6 straight on, ignoring a crossing path and eventually emerging from the wood with a barbed-wire fence in front of you. Here turn right and follow a fenced path which widens into a green lane and leads you to South Stoke Road in Woodcote. Turn left onto this and follow it for just over a quarter mile to your starting point.

Walk A also continues downhill along the outside edge of Dean Wood, but stays outside the sunken gully, rounding a protruding corner of the wood and eventually reaching the fence of an orchard at Dean Farm. Here turn left and follow this fence to its far end, then turn left onto path WD5 between hedges. After a quarter mile, cross a stile and bear slightly right, gradually climbing through a belt of trees into the right-hand field. On entering the field, follow a left-hand hedge straight on to a corner where you go through a hedge gap and step over a pig-wire fence, then turn right and follow a right-hand hedge uphill with a fine view of the Berkshire Downs to your left. Where the hedge turns right, leave it and follow what is normally a crop-break straight on uphill to a footbridge leading to the A4074.

Turn left along its verge, then at the start of a layby, cross the main road and take a grassy track opposite (bridleway C37, later IP21), following it downhill to a junction of minor roads in the valley bottom. Here take a narrow road straight on uphill. At the top of the rise, turn right onto another narrow macadam road called Braziers Lane with glimpses of Braziers Park, a late seventeenth-century mansion with castellated Regency wings through the left-hand hedge and follow it for half a mile. Where its macadam surface ends by a cottage, take its stony continuation (IP15) straight on, climbing gradually and entering Itchen Wood. Near the top of the hill, where woodland also commences to the left and the track bears left, leave it and take path C7 straight on along the contours of the hill for about 200 yards, looking out for a steeply descending path to the right with a flight of steps and a handrail. Turn right here onto path C6, following it steeply downhill to a stile into a field where a fine view opens out of the peaceful

IPSDEN

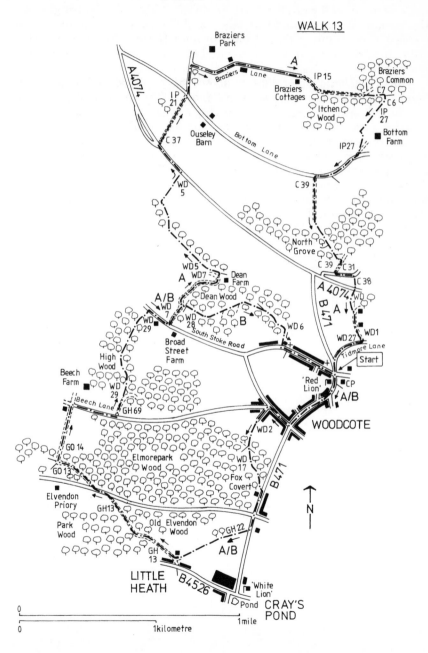

WALK 13

Braziers
Park

Braziers Lane

IP 15

Braziers
Cottages

Braziers
Common

C7
C6

Itchen
Wood

IP
27

IP
21

Bottom Lane

Bottom
Farm

A4074

C 37

Ouseley
Barn

IP27

WD
5

C 39

North
Grove

C 39
C 31

C 38

WD5
WD7

Dean
Farm

A

A4074

WD

A/B

Dean Wood

A

WD
7

B

B471

WD
28

WD
29

South Stoke Road

WD 6

WD 27
WD1

Tidmore Lane

Start

Broad
Street
Farm

+

+

High
Wood

'Red
Lion'

CP

Beech
Farm

WD
29

A/B

Beech Lane

GH69

WOODCOTE

WD2

GO 14

B471

Elmorepark
Wood

WD
17

GO 13

Fox
Covert

Elvendon
Priory

GH13

Park
Wood

Old Elvendon
Wood

GH 22

N

GH
13

A/B

LITTLE
HEATH

B4526

'White
Lion'

Pond

CRAY'S
POND

0

0   1kilometre   1mile

69

Chiltern coombe around Bottom Farm. Cross this stile and take path IP27, bearing half right across the field to a stile then go straight on to the corner of a post-and-rail fence and follow it to a stile. Having crossed this, follow a fenced path around Bottom Farm to a further stile, then bear right across a paddock to a stile in its far corner leading to Bottom Lane.

Turn right onto this road and about 150 yards beyond a right-hand bend, turn left onto a grassy track (path C39) and follow it climbing gently to a stile by some gates. Having crossed this stile, bear slightly left to a gate and stile into a wood called North Grove. Inside the wood follow an obvious path straight on, ignoring a branching path to the right, then, where the path forks, take a lesser path straight on to reach the edge of the wood by a gas pipe marker post and follow a fence to the corner of the field. Here turn right onto a crossing track and follow it to a gate and stile leading to a narrow road (C31). Turn left onto this and after 150 yards, at a left-hand bend, turn right over a stile onto path C38. Now follow a left-hand hedge to cross a stile onto the A4074. Cross this road and a stile opposite and take fenced path WD1 to a stile onto a drive. Cross the stile and a drive, then go straight on through a fence gap and take another drive straight on to a narrow road called Tidmore Lane (WD27). Turn right onto this road and follow it to the B471, where you turn left for your starting point.

WALK 14: Goring-on-Thames

Length of Walk: 8.3 miles / 13.3 Km

Starting Point: Entrance to Goring & Streatley Station.

Grid Ref: SU603806

Maps: OS Landranger Sheets 174 & 175
OS Explorer Sheet 171
OS Pathfinder Sheets 1155 (SU48/58), 1156 (SU68/78)
(or old Explorer Sheet 3), 1171 (SU47/57) &
1172 (SU67/77)
Chiltern Society FP Map No. 16

How to get there / Parking: Goring-on-Thames, 8 miles
north-west of Reading, may be reached from the town by
taking the A329 towards Wallingford to Streatley. Here
turn right onto the B4009, crossing the Thames into
Goring. There is a small public car park behind the
'Catherine Wheel' in Station Road and another at the
railway station, but on-street parking is inadvisable in
the narrow streets of the town centre.

Goring-on-Thames, although in some ways resembling other
Thames-side Chiltern towns, has a number of unique features
arising from its geographical location. Situated in the Goring
Gap which separates two ranges of chalk hills, the Chilterns
and the Berkshire Downs, where these two ranges drop
steeply into the Thames Valley, Goring has a scenically
spectacular setting. This is enhanced by the wealth of trees on
both sides of the river and a number of islands in the river
itself. Goring is also of considerable historic interest as it is
the point at which the ancient Icknield Way crossed the
Thames well before Roman times. It can boast a substantially
unaltered eleventh-century church built by Robert d'Oilly,
containing a bell cast in 1290 and believed to be the oldest in
Britain and a number of highly attractive inns and cottages
including the sixteenth-century 'Miller of Mansfield'.

The walk, one of the finest in the Chilterns, follows the
Thames for much of the way from Goring to Whitchurch,
partly on the towpath and partly on an elevated terraced path
through Hartslock Wood, now a nature reserve. It returns over
Whitchurch Hill and via Upper Gatehampton Farm with
superb panoramic views of the Thames Valley before it
descends into Goring.

Starting from the entrance to Goring and Streatley Station, follow the road northwards to reach a bridge over the railway. Turn left here onto the B4009, crossing to its other pavement and follow it straight on down the High Street. Just past Lloyds Bank and the Post Office, turn left onto fenced macadam path G03, passing a car park and emerging into Station Road by the 'Catherine Wheel'. Turn right along this road and where it turns sharp right, go straight on down Ferry Lane, which is believed to be the ancient route of the Icknield Way down to the Thames. At the end of the road, take path GO3a straight on between anti-vehicle barriers and across a green to the bank of the Thames. Turn left here onto the towpath (GO26, at one point ST24), joining the Thames Path and follow it for 1.3 miles, at one point passing under graceful brick Gatehampton railway bridge built by the renowned Great Western Railway builder, Isambard Kingdom Brunel.

On reaching Ferry Cottage, where the towpath transfers to the Berkshire bank, turn left onto fenced path GO30 to a footbridge. At this point, at the time of writing, it is necessary to take a *de facto* path which is subject to alteration. Walkers are advised to heed any signs or waymarks. The *de facto* path crosses the footbridge and follows a left-hand fence straight on to reach a crossing fenced bridleway (GO7) near the 'lost village' of Gatehampton to your left. Turn right here (now back on an official route) and follow this fenced bridleway, looking out for Basildon's thirteenth-century church through the trees to your right on the other side of the Thames. This is where the original Jethro Tull, the eighteenth-century inventor of the seed-drill, is buried. On entering Hartslock Wood, continue straight on for three-quarters of a mile on a path which soon becomes a terrace cut into the side of a steep slope dropping into the Thames. Near the far end of the wood, the path climbs higher and swings away from the Thames and on leaving the wood, follow fenced bridleway GH7, dropping steeply into a hollow, then climb a flight of steps (now on WH11) to join a rough road. Go straight on along this for three-quarters of a mile, ignoring all side turnings until you reach the B471 on the outskirts of Whitchurch.

Whitchurch and Pangbourne, on the other side of the Thames, are both worth exploring, especially in view of their beautiful riverside setting. If wishing to explore these villages or seek refreshments, turn right; otherwise, leaving the Thames Path, cross the road and turn left along a raised roadside pathway climbing Whitchurch Hill. Where this pathway ends, cross the road again by the war memorial and just before a right-hand bend, leave the road and take a sloping path straight on uphill to a kissing-gate. Go through this and take path GH27 straight on, following the outside edge of a wood called Stonycroft Plantation until you reach a gate and kissing-gate into a fenced lane. Go straight on along this lane and on reaching Beech Farm, follow the track swinging right of the buildings. Now cross a concrete drive and go through a small gate, then follow a left-hand fence to a kissing-gate into Beech Wood. Follow the obvious path through the wood to a fork. Here bear half left onto path GH26 which crosses the wood to a stile into a field. Go straight on across the field, heading towards a barn with a tiled roof at Coombe End Farm. Cross a stile and then continue to a gate into the farmyard. Enter this, soon turning right and going through a gate into a field. Now turn left to a stile and gate into a lane at Coombe End, onto which you turn right.

On reaching a macadam road, turn left onto it. At a fork by a pair of cottages, go right and continue for a further quarter mile until a view of Goring Gap opens out ahead. Here, where the road wiggles to the right, leave it and take a sunken green lane straight on. After some 180 yards, on reaching a branching track by a left-hand gate, turn right onto the track (path GO25) through a hedge gap to join a private macadam road. Follow this straight on, soon bearing left with fine views of the Goring Gap ahead and to your left. On reaching some farm buildings, the road (and path GO25) bear right between buildings to a T-junction. Here turn left onto bridleway GO17a, a farm road to and through Upper Gatehampton Farm.

Having passed through the farm, just before entering a copse, turn right over a stile by a gate onto path GO17, crossing a second stile left of a stable and a third by the corner of a garden. Now continue between a fence and hedge to a fourth stile. Here go straight on to the right-hand end of a hedge, then turn right and by the corner of a barn to your right, turn left through an old gateway into a field and cross the field diagonally to a stile into Great Chalk Wood. Inside the wood, at a junction of tracks, take a wide grassy track straight on. Now ignore a crossing track, after which your track narrows and reaches a T-junction. Here turn sharp left onto another track (path GO16) and follow it, disregarding a crossing track, a branching track to your right and later a branching track to your left. Where the track finally turns sharp left, leave it and take a waymarked path straight on, eventually leaving the wood by a stile. Now go straight on through thick scrub to a further stile, then turn right and follow a right-hand hedge uphill. At the top corner of the field, turn left and follow a right-hand hedge along the top edge of two fields, gradually dropping into the Thames Valley. At the far end of the second field, ignore a gate and stile to your right and go straight on through a hedge gap, then follow a right-hand fence to a stile in it. Cross this and bear slightly left across a recreation ground to a gate leading to a spacious residential road. Now follow this road, swinging left then right, then turn left onto the B4526 which leads you back to your starting point.

WALK 15:   Whitchurch Hill

Length of Walk: (A)   7.3 miles / 11.8 Km
                             (B)   7.8 miles / 12.6 Km

Starting Point: Road junction at southern corner of
Whitchurch Hill village recreation ground.

Grid Ref: SU638787

Maps: OS Landranger Sheet 175
OS Explorer Sheet 171
OS Pathfinder Sheets 1156 (SU68/78)
(or old Explorer Sheet 3) & 1171 (SU67/77)
Chiltern Society FP Map No. 16

How to get there/Parking: Whitchurch Hill, nearly 6 miles
north-west of Reading, may be reached from the town by
taking the A329 towards Wallingford and Oxford to
Pangbourne. Now turn right onto the B471, crossing
Whitchurch Toll Bridge and continuing for a further
1.2 miles to a road junction at the top of Whitchurch Hill.
Here fork right onto a road signposted to Goring Heath
and after about 200 yards, park in a roadside parking area
on your left by the village recreation ground.

Whitchurch Hill, on the edge of the upland plateau above the
Thames Valley, is a village of relatively modern origin. Before
1813 it merely consisted of a few farms and cottages on the
edge of a vast upland heath known as Whitchurch Common
and Goring Heath, but following the inclosure of Whitchurch
Common in that year and that of Goring Heath in 1812, the
village grew and in more recent years substantial 'in-filling'
development has taken place to produce the mixture of
predominantly Victorian and modern architecture which we
find there today.

The walk leads you from this albeit pleasant outpost of
suburbia through the heavily-wooded area to the north and
east to the hamlet of Nuney Green before a spectacular drop
into a Thames-side coombe brings you to the secluded and
picturesque riverside village of Mapledurham which is
nevertheless steeped in history. The return route takes you
along the Thames Valley to Hardwick House, another historic
mansion, before climbing through woodland to Path Hill and
continuing across the plateau to Whitchurch Hill.

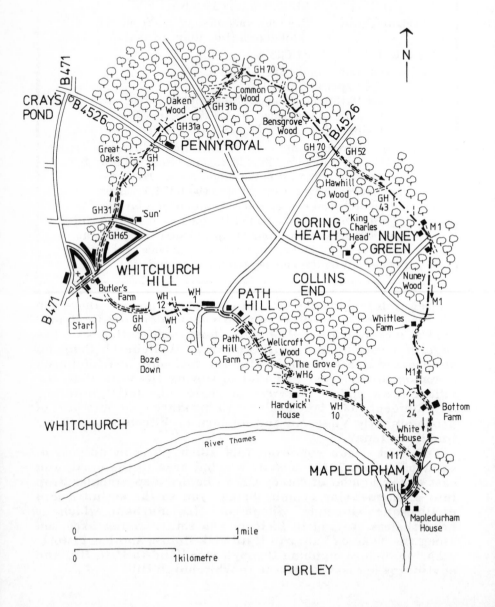

WOODCOTE

WALK 15

B471

CRAYS POND

B4526

Oaken Wood

GH 70

Common Wood

GH 31b

GH 31a

Bensgrove Wood

PENNYROYAL

B4526

GH 70

GH 52

Great Oaks

GH 31

Hawhill Wood

GH 43

N

GH31

'Sun'

GORING HEATH

'King Charles Head'

NUNEY GREEN

M1

GH65

WHITCHURCH HILL

WH 1

PATH HILL

COLLINS END

Nuney Wood

M1

Butler's Farm

WH 12

Whittles Farm

B471

Start

GH 60

WH 1

Path Hill Farm

Wellcroft Wood

The Grove

WH6

M1

Boze Down

M 24

Bottom Farm

WHITCHURCH

Hardwick House

WH 10

White House

M17

MAPLEDURHAM

River Thames

Mill

Mapledurham House

0   1 mile

0   1 kilometre

PURLEY

76

Starting from the road junction at the southern corner of the village recreation ground at Whitchurch Hill, take the Goring Heath road northeastwards past the recreation ground and Butler's Farm with its large pond. Just past a telephone box, turn left into Bridle Road (bridleway GH65) and follow this rough lane straight on, gradually narrowing to a normal bridleway. After a third of a mile, cross a road and take a rough lane (bridleway GH31) straight on past some houses, then between hedges to a gate and gap into a wood called Great Oaks. Inside the wood, fork immediately right onto a path following its inside edge. Disregard a crossing track and branching paths to the left and continue until you reach a concrete road. Turn right onto this and follow it to a gate onto the B4526 near the woodland hamlet of Pennyroyal.

Cross this road and take bridleway GH31a straight on through Oaken Wood for over a third of a mile, ignoring all crossing or branching tracks or paths, until you reach another road known as Long Toll, which, despite its name, was never a turnpike road. Having crossed this, take bridleway GH31b straight on through Common Wood for a third of a mile, ignoring two major crossing tracks. At a waymarked crossways near the corner of a field to your left, turn right onto waymarked bridleway GH70. After a quarter mile, ignore a crossing bridleway and bear half right onto a waymarked path. This path soon joins another and bears slightly left onto it. Disregard a waymarked branching path to the right, then, about 80 yards further on, follow the waymarks turning left. Where the waymarked path then turns right, follow it, ignoring a branching path to the left and continuing through Bensgrove Wood for a further third of a mile to the B4526. Cross this road again and take bridleway GH52 virtually opposite straight on through Hawhill Wood, soon with fields coming into view to your left. Where woodland recommences to your left, ignore a crossing path and take bridleway GH43 straight on, soon with a narrow field to your left. At the far end of this field pass left of the first woodland pond and right of the second then follow a left-hand boundary bank straight on until the bridleway (now M1) becomes enclosed between hedges and leads you to a rough lane at the woodland hamlet of Nuney Green.

Bear half right onto this lane and follow it straight on past the end of a macadam road, then, at the far end of the garden of a right-hand bungalow, turn right onto path M1 between hedges which leads you into Nuney Wood. In the wood take an obvious sunken path straight on, eventually reaching a stile into a field. Cross this and go straight on between a fence and a line of trees to reach a gate and stile onto a road. Turn right onto this road, then immediately left onto the drive to Whittles Farm (still path M1). By the farm, follow a rough lane straight on, soon bending left with views of the Thames Valley opening out ahead. On reaching a stile in the right-hand fence, cross it and follow a left-hand hedge, later a fence, straight on downhill through two fields to reach the end of a farm road in the valley bottom near Bottom Farm. Turn left onto this farm road (bridleway M24) and follow it through the farm and on to reach a bend in the public road to Mapledurham. Turn right onto this road and follow it to 'The White House'. If wishing to visit the fascinating village of Mapledurham, continue straight on for a further quarter mile into the village; otherwise omit the next paragraph.

Mapledurham, the name of which is derived from the Saxon 'Mapledreham', meaning 'homestead by the maple tree', was once a very leafy place, until, in the 1970s, Dutch elm disease decimated its tree population. Along the village street are a number of seventeenth-century cottages including a row of almshouses. At its far end on the right is the fifteenth-century Mapledurham Mill with its wooden tower, the oldest mill on the Thames. To the left is the church, built in about 1200 with the tower heightened in extensive renovations in 1862. An interesting feature of this otherwise Protestant church is a screened-off Catholic chapel belonging to the Eystons, heirs of the Blount family, the traditionally Catholic owners of the Mapledurham Estate. Behind the church is Mapledurham House, part of which is a timber-framed fifteenth-century building, but much of which was rebuilt in brick by Sir Michael Blount in 1588. This house was visited when new by Elizabeth I and made famous by John Galsworthy who names it as the home of Soames in his 'Forsyte Saga'. Alexander Pope, the satirist, also visited it and befriended Martha Blount. Now retrace your steps to 'The White House'.

By 'The White House', take fenced bridleway M17 northwestwards for over half a mile, with fine views of the Thames Valley both ahead and behind, until you reach the ornamental, wrought-iron lodge gates of Hardwick Park. Now follow a rough track (bridleway WH10) straight on for some 700 yards, keeping right at a fork and passing Hardwick House to your left. Built on foundations dating from about 1400, the present house with its Elizabethan chimneys and mullioned windows dates principally from the time of the Tudor politician, Richard Lybbe who also entertained Queen Elizabeth I there. Where the lane bears left and joins the macadam drive to Hardwick House, turn right onto bridleway WH6, a fenced track leading uphill into a wood called The Grove. Inside the wood, fork right, climbing gently then rounding a sharp left-hand bend by a chalkpit and continuing uphill for nearly a quarter mile. Near the top, ignore a major crossing track and go straight on through Wellcroft Wood, disregarding two branching tracks to the right and a crossing track. On leaving the wood, continue along a lane to reach the end of a road by Path Hill Farm. Now follow this road straight on to a junction by some cottages at Path Hill where you turn left. At a left-hand bend where the road starts to drop, fork right onto a gravel drive (path WH1). At the end of the drive, go straight on over a stile and follow the top hedge of the field to a stile leading to a fenced track (WH12). Turn left onto this track and on reaching a hedge, turn right over a stile onto path WH1, following a left-hand hedge, later a fence, wiggling to the right at one point, to reach a gap in a line of trees. Here take path GH60 straight on along a farm track beside a right-hand fence. On reaching a copse, the track becomes enclosed between fences, then, about 120 yards beyond the copse, turn left through a kissing-gate and bear half right across a field to reach a kissing-gate left of a row of cottages at Whitchurch Hill. Go through this gate and follow a fenced path past the cottages to reach a road near your starting point.

WALK 16: Highmoor Cross

Length of Walk: 5.6 miles / 9.1 Km

Starting Point: Small green near the church at Highmoor Cross.

Grid Ref: SU700844

Maps: OS Landranger Sheet 175
OS Explorer Sheet 171 (or old Sheet 3)
OS Pathfinder Sheet 1156 (SU68/78)
Chiltern Society FP Map No. 2

How to get there / Parking: Highmoor Cross, 4 miles west of Henley-on-Thames, may be reached from the town by taking the A4130 towards Oxford. At a roundabout just before Nettlebed, turn left onto the B481 towards Reading. A quarter mile past the 'Dog and Duck', turn right into the turning signposted to Witheridge Hill, Stoke Row and Checkendon, where there is a small car park behind the bus shelter on the triangle of grass immediately to your left.

Notes: Heavy nettle growth may be encountered on paths HM2 and HM11 in the summer months.

Highmoor, which consists of two hamlets a quarter mile apart, Highmoor Cross and Highmoor, is set in a heavily wooded location on the Reading to Nettlebed road in the heart of the Oxfordshire Chilterns. Like neighbouring Stoke Row, the village would seem to be of relatively recent origin, scattered along a road in a woodland clearing. This is suggested by the fact that both Highmoor and Stoke Row were shown on the 1830 Ordnance Survey map as only a few scattered cottages and, prior to 1952, both were merely upland parts of some of the 'strip parishes' on the slopes from the Thames into the Chilterns – in Highmoor's case, Rotherfield Greys; in Stoke Row's, Ipsden, Newnham Murren and Mongewell. Both also have only had churches since Victorian times.

Much of the walk goes through woodland of various types interspersed with quiet pockets of farmland, mainly pasture. The larger village of Stoke Row with its oriental oddity, the Maharajah's Well, and its abundance of cherry trees is also visited.

Starting from the green near the church at Highmoor Cross, take the B481 northwards towards Nettlebed. Having passed the 'Dog and Duck', turn left onto path HM4, the drive to 'Appletree Cottage', and bear right between hedges to a stile. Cross this and follow the left-hand hedge to another stile into a wood. Just inside the wood, fork right through some holly bushes. At a waymarked junction take path HM2 bearing half right, crossing one macadam drive and joining a second. Bear slightly left onto this, disregarding two branches to the left and one to the right and soon passing under two archways. Beyond these, the path continues straight on through a hedge gap and then a gate into another wood. Follow the obvious path straight on through the wood and over a stile into a field. Ignoring a second stile into the field to the right, follow the right-hand fence downhill to a stile into Nott Wood. Inside the wood, follow an ill-defined path bearing slightly right, until you reach a well-defined crossing path. Turn right onto this and now on path NU26 follow it with a plantation to your left, until the path forks. Here go right, dropping down through some mature beech trees, then turn left along a slight gully which crosses the path, soon with an obvious boundary bank to your left. Follow this bank uphill, disregarding a branching path to your right, until you reach a crossing track. Turn left onto this and follow it to a rough lane at the edge of the wood.

Here turn left onto this lane (bridleway SR37) and follow it through the wood for nearly a quarter mile. Beyond the far end of the plantation to your right, on rounding a left-hand bend where a field becomes visible to your right, turn right onto path SR27 following the inside edge of the wood to a stile in the corner of the wood leading into a field. Cross this stile, ignore a gate to your right and bear right following a right-hand hedge through two fields to gates at Newnham Hill Farm, the name of which reflects the fact that this was formerly part of the Thames-side 'strip parish' of Newnham Murren. Go through these gates and follow a fenced lane straight on. On rounding a pond to your left, go right at a fork. At a second fork where the road to the left becomes macadamed, take the narrow fenced path SR27 straight on into woodland and downhill to the road in the valley bottom. Turn right onto this road and after about 40 yards turn left onto path SR34 into Bush Wood, soon passing through a gap by a gate. Ignore a branching path to the left and go straight on through the wood until you reach a gate and stile. Now bear slightly left across a paddock climbing to a stile in its top right-hand corner. Having crossed this, go straight on to a gap between the 'Crooked Billet' and a barn to reach Nottwood Lane.

Turn right onto this road and follow it to a sharp left-hand bend. Here leave the road by a kissing-gate on the right and take path SR3, following a right-hand hedge through a cottage garden and adjoining paddock and negotiating a series of stiles and gates. At the far end of the paddock, cross a stile by a gate and a second stile under a hawthorn tree. Now continue along the other side of the hedge to two gates. Go through these and follow the left-hand fence uphill to another gate by Stokerow Farm. Turn left through this and follow a concrete, later macadam, farm road straight on through three more gates to the end of a public road. Turn left along the road and follow it for 350 yards, until you reach a narrow hedged path to the right with a white horse barrier across its end. Turn right onto this path (SR2) and follow it out to the main road at Stoke Row.

The most interesting feature of Stoke Row is the Maharajah's Well which you see to your right just before reaching the road. This 368 feet deep well with its oriental canopy was given to the village by the Maharajah of Benares in 1864 as a token of thanks to Sir Edward Reade of Ipsden House for services rendered to his province and was in use till the 1950s when piped water came to Stoke Row.

Turn right along the road, then, just before reaching the church, turn left into School Lane. Just before the last pair of houses on the left, turn left again onto fenced path SR22 which leads you into Common Wood. In the wood, bear slightly right and follow the obvious path SR23, soon passing a modern house to reach a road. Cross this road and continue straight on through the wood to a second road. Turn right onto this road, rounding a left-hand bend. After a few yards, turn right onto a stony track (bridleway C2) and follow the track through the wood and then between fields to reach Neal's Lane at Neal's Farm. Turn left onto this road and follow it, re-entering the woods and then emerging into a clearing where a road junction is reached by Hinds Farm.

Here turn left, then immediately fork right onto path P1 into a wood called Burnt Platt, following a right-hand fence past a wooden bungalow. After a while, pass an underground reservoir to the right. Now follow the obvious path, bearing left away from the fence, through a gate and past a plantation. Disregard a crossing fire break, a track which emerges from the plantation and a wide crossing track and take bridleway P2 straight on, soon passing through a fence gap into mature woodland. Here ignore a branching bridleway to the left and take bridleway HM29 straight on. Where it starts to descend, disregard a fork to the right and follow the path which curves first left and then right, until you reach a rough road at the edge of the wood. Turn right onto this and follow it past a field to your left. At the far end of the field, turn left over a stile and take path HM9 downhill along the inside edge of Greyhone Wood to a path junction in the valley bottom. Here turn left onto path HM11 which leads you between

WALK 16

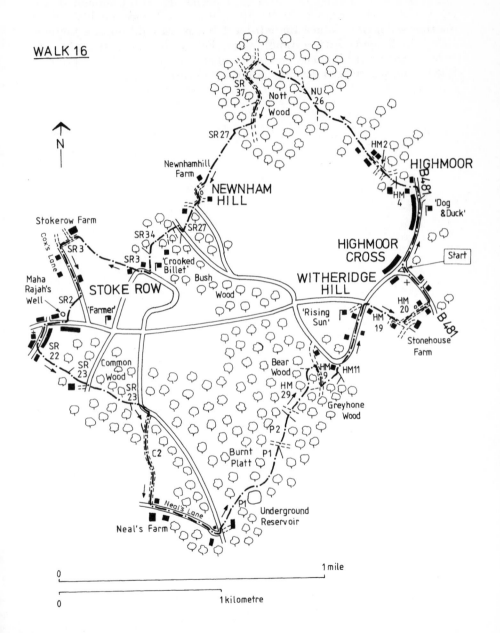

hedges to a bend in a road. Turn right onto this road and follow it uphill to a road junction on the edge of Witheridge Hill Common. Turn right over a stile onto path HM19, going uphill between hedges to another stile. Here follow the left-hand hedge straight on to a further stile which leads into a rough lane. Follow the lane straight on, turning left where it turns and continuing (now on path HM20) to the B481 road, where your starting point is 300 yards to the left.

WALK 17:   Rotherfield Peppard

Length of Walk: 7.8 miles / 12.6 Km
Starting Point: Rotherfield Peppard Church of England
Primary School.
Grid Ref: SU710816
Maps: OS Landranger Sheet 175
OS Explorer Sheet 171
OS Pathfinder Sheets 1156 (SU68/78) (or old Explorer
Sheet 3) & 1172 (SU67/77)
Chiltern Society FP Map No. 4
How to get there / Parking: Rotherfield Peppard, 5 miles
north of Reading, may be reached from the town by taking
the A4155 towards Henley across the Thames to
Coversham, then forking left onto the B481 towards
Nettlebed. Follow this for 4.5 miles until, at the top of a
steep winding hill, you reach a signpost to Peppard
Church. Turn right here and look for a parking space,
bearing in mind that for the sake of local residents and
future visitors, it is advisable to avoid obstructing
gateways or parking on mown frontages.

Rotherfield Peppard, with its extensive common straddling
the Reading to Nettlebed road, is rather a scattered
community. Its houses are ranged about the common, the main
group being in the area on the east side around the lane to the
parish church. Despite its proximity to the large residential
sprawl of Sonning Common, a modern satellite of nearby
Reading, the village has managed to preserve its rural charm
and identity. As with many villages, its most interesting
building is the twelfth-century church with its tower and
steeple, for the preservation of which the village is indebted to
Mrs Mirabelle Grey, who, in the early part of this century,
encouraged its restoration and donated much of the internal
woodwork.

The walk, which passes the church and circles Sonning
Common taking in Crowsley Park and Kidmore End with its
picturesque village centre, traverses peaceful gently rolling
hills and valleys dropping down towards the Thames as well
as some characteristic Chiltern beechwoods.

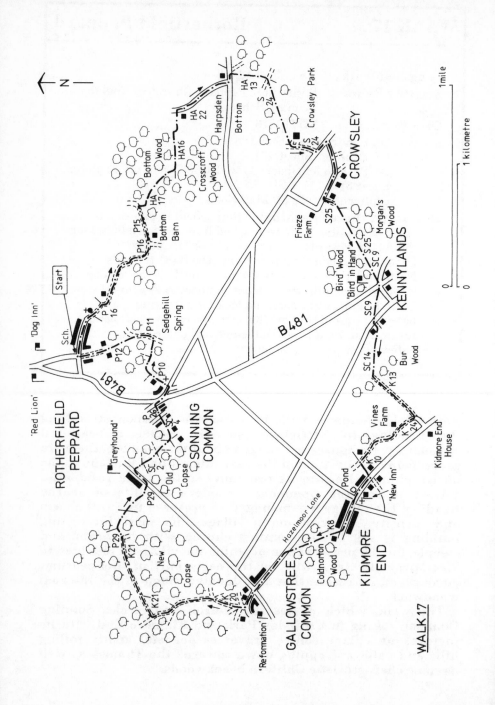

WALK17

86

Starting from the Church of England Primary School in Church Lane, Rotherfield Peppard, follow Church Lane eastwards to the church. Bear right of the church and continue along a rough lane (path P16). At the end of the lane, turn right to enter a field, then turn left and follow the left-hand hedge passing a cottage. After some 350 yards at the far end of the field turn right beside a belt of trees to the corner of a copse. Now turn left onto a grassy track through the belt of trees and follow the edge of the copse, then bear left beside a hedge to the remains of a farm known as Bottom Barn. Continue straight on along the track (now bridleway P15) past the site of the farm and beside a fence until you reach a corner of Bottom Wood. Here turn right over two stiles onto path HA17 entering the wood, then take an obvious path which soon turns left and follows a firebreak through a plantation. At one point, ignore a branching path to the left, then, on reaching a wire fence which prevents passage forward, turn left onto crossing path HA16 which follows the fence steeply uphill to a stile into a field. Now follow the right-hand hedge straight on and, just before the far end of the field, transfer through a gap then cross a rail-stile and take a fenced path along the other side of the hedge past a house to reach a macadam lane (HA22). Turn right onto this and follow it downhill into Harpsden Bottom.

Here you reach another road by the attractive gabled Old Place, formerly Bottomhouse Farm. Turn left onto this road and after a few yards, turn right over a ladder stile onto path HA13 entering Crowsley Park. Walking at right angles to the road, make for a small marker post ahead. Having reached this, go straight on, heading left of a distant cedar, to arrive at another marker post by a disused raised track. Here fork right onto path S24 and, passing between a cedar to your left and a storm-damaged oak to your right, make for a stile by a group of large chestnut trees. Cross this stile and go straight on to another stile at the left-hand end of an avenue of chestnut trees, where you have a close-up view to your left of Crowsley Park House, a large red-brick Jacobean house. Now keep straight on past the house to a macadam drive. Turn left onto this drive and, ignoring two branches to the left, follow it to the lodge house and through the lodge gates to a road.

Turn left onto the road and follow it until you reach a turning on the right signposted to Crowsley. Take this turning and ignoring turnings to the left, follow the road for a third of a mile past several cottages including a thatched cottage on the left-hand side. Just past this, turn left into a rough lane (path S25). At the end of the lane, cross a stile by a gate and bear slightly right across a field to a stile at a corner of Morgan's Wood. Cross this and follow the outside edge of the wood to another corner, then go straight on across the field to a pair of stiles between the right-hand-most trees in a hedge in a dip ahead. Continue straight on over these stiles and across the next field (now on path SC9) to cross another stile in the trees ahead. A few yards through the trees a road is reached. Turn right here and follow the road out to the 'Bird in Hand' crossroads.

Here cross the B481, go through a kissing-gate opposite and, still on path SC9, bear half-right following a worn path to a kissing-gate in the hedge ahead leading to Kennylands Road. Now take path SC14, a rough fenced drive right of the house opposite. By double gates into a garden, fork half right, keeping left of the corner of a fence ahead and following a fenced path to a stile. Cross this and continue straight on across a field to a gate and stile into Bur Wood. Having crossed the stile, take path K13 following a farm track through the trees and then beside a fence, until you reach a gate and stile leading to a right-angle bend on macadam lane K24, where Kidmore End House can be seen ahead. Turn right into this lane and follow it part Vine Farm, where the original timber-framed house has, at some time, been extended in brick and flint. Here the macadam surface ends and you continue along a rough lane. Having passed Emmens Cottage, an attractive gabled building on the right, turn left over a stile onto path K10. Cross a field to a stile and continue between fences to the village street at Kidmore End, then turn right onto it towards the centre of the village.

The centre of Kidmore End with its pond, well, pub, sixteenth-century half-timbered houses and early Victorian church clustered around a crossroads, is still a village of rural charm. At the crossroads, continue straight on until, near the end of the village, you reach a chestnut tree on the left. Here turn right into the drive of a house called Norton Lee and fork immediately left onto path K8, a hedged path with a horse barrier. Now follow the path which later crosses a field and goes straight on through Coldnorton Wood to join Hazelmoor Lane. Bear left onto this road and follow it to a crossroads at Gallowstree Common.

Cross this crossroads and continue straight on along a road called The Hamlet. At a sharp left-hand bend by the corner of a wood called New Copse, turn right into the wood. Just inside the wood, bear half left onto path K20, the centre track of a three-way fork, and at a further fork a few yards further on, bear half right. After some 200 yards, fork left by a tree with two trunks and follow a waymarked track, ignoring a crossing firebreak and other crossing or branching tracks, until you reach a gap in a boundary bank near a woodland pond and the corner of a field ahead. Here turn right onto path K21 and follow this obvious path, later a track alongside the boundary bank for nearly half a mile. Where, just past a large pit, the track forks right away from the bank, take path P29, continuing to follow the bank to a stile into a field. Cross this stile and follow a left-hand hedge, ignoring a stile in it and reaching a stile near a gate in a crossing fence. Having crossed this, go straight on to the corner of a hedge by a new house, then follow this hedge straight on to a road.

Turn left onto the road and on reaching a well, turn right into a wood called Old Copse. Here take path SC2, a winding waymarked path, through the wood for nearly a quarter mile, ignoring all crossing or branching tracks. Shortly before reaching the far side of the wood, near the end of a wire-mesh fence, turn sharp left onto a more worn path (SC3), then turn immediately right onto path SC4 which leads you to a corner of the wood and continues as path P26 down an alleyway to a road in Shiplake Bottom. Cross this and continue up another alleyway, climbing steps at one point, to reach Stoke Row Road. Turn right onto this road, then cross the B481 into Blounts Court Road. Just past a turning called Priory Copse, turn left onto narrow hedged path P10 leading into a wood. Now ignore paths branching first to the left, then the right and then the left again and follow the path to a bricked spring called Sedgehill Spring. Just past this, turn left onto path P11, a woodland track downhill, leaving the wood and following its outside edge. Where the track turns right, leave it and take path P12 straight on through a wire gate, then bearing half right uphill to a stile. Having crossed this, follow a fenced path uphill through a plantation to reach Spring Wood Lane which leads you out to Peppard Common near your starting point.

WALK 18:   Sonning Eye

Length of Walk: 6.6 miles / 10.6 Km

Starting Point: Sharp bend in Sonning Eye village road.

Grid Ref: SU750760

Maps: OS Landranger Sheet 175
            OS Explorer Sheets 159 or 171
            OS Pathfinder Sheet 1172 (SU67/77)
            Chiltern Society FP Map No. 4

How to get there / Parking: Sonning Eye, 2.5 miles
northeast of Reading, may be reached from the town by
taking the A4155 towards Henley-on-Thames to a
roundabout at Play Hatch. Here turn right onto the B478
towards Sonning. At the next roundabout, turn right for
Sonning Eye, following the road round a sharp right-hand
bend and parking in this cul-de-sac road, taking care not
to obstruct entrances or turning provisions.

Notes: Several sections of this walk are prone to heavy nettle
growth in the summer months.

Sonning Eye, at the Oxfordshire end of Sonning Bridge, has
both a picturesque riverside setting and a number of
attractive buildings largely not noticed by the passing
motorist on the B478. The village name, which is thought to
mean Sonning Island, suggests that before man sought to
control the flow of the River Thames, the very flat area on
which the village is built may have been a large island in the
river. Its name also points to an interesting historical anomaly
in that, although this village and a large tract of land
extending northwestwards for nearly five miles to beyond
Sonning Common have always been in Oxfordshire, they
traditionally belonged to the parish of Sonning, whose mother
village has always been in Berkshire. This anomaly was
abolished in the late nineteenth-century, when, as a part of the
extensive Victorian reforms which set up the modern local
government structure, the Oxfordshire part of the parish was
made into the separate parish of Eye and Dunsden and
subsequently the northern part, where the modern satellite
village of Sonning Common had grown up, also became an
independent parish. However, reminders still persist not only
in place names but also in the fact that the parish records for

the whole ancient parish of Sonning are located in the Berkshire county archives.

The walk, which is of an easy nature, first explores the village before taking you along the beautiful, peaceful section of towpath to Shiplake, where a short climb leads you onto the low hills north of the river valley where fine views across it can be obtained in places. Your return route takes you across these hills with a characteristic Chiltern mixture of farmland and woods before descending, with superb panoramic views to the south, back into Sonning Eye.

Starting from the sharp right-hand bend in the Sonning Eye village road, take the narrow road to the left into the village, following it round a sharp bend by an attractive thatched barn. Now, by the parish noticeboard, turn right onto fenced macadam path ED13 which leads you to join the B478 opposite the 'French Horn'. Here turn right, crossing the new backwater bridges, then, by the traffic lights at the Oxfordshire end of the main river bridge, joining the Thames Path, turn left onto path ED20, the Thames towpath, crossing a footbridge and continuing along the riverbank for two miles (later on path S28). On reaching a boathouse of Shiplake College, cross a raised footbridge, then turn sharp left onto bridleway S9, (joining the reverse direction of Walk 19) taking a rough track left of further boathouses away from the river into woodland. At a crossways, turn right onto a narrow fenced bridleway climbing a series of steps and eventually emerging in a vehicular turning area by Shiplake Church.

Built in about 1140 and enlarged in the thirteenth century, this church is best known as being where the poet Tennyson married in 1850. It also boasts a wealth of fifteenth-century French stained glass from the ruined Benedictine Abbey of St. Bertin in St. Omer. The glass was buried for safety during the French Revolution and later sold when the Order was suppressed.

Here bear half left through a gate into Church Lane and follow this road past the church to a crossroads with the A4155 by the 'Plowden Arms'. Cross the main road carefully and take the Binfield Heath road straight on. After passing its second junction with Plowden Way, turn left at a right-hand bend onto path S10, a concrete farm road. Where the concrete road turns left, go straight on through a kissing-gate and along a grass track across fields, with wide views across the Thames Valley to your left, to cross a stile. At this point, at the time of writing, it is necessary to take a *de facto* path which is subject to alteration. Walkers are advised to heed any signs or waymarks. Here the *de facto* route turns right and follows a right-hand fence to its end, then turns left along what is usually a crop break, passing a clump of bushes (where you part company again with Walk 19) and continuing under a power-line to the next telegraph pole. Here you rejoin the official path and bear half right across the field to a hedge gap leading into a green lane. Go through this gap, cross the green lane and go straight on through a further gap, heading just left of a group of conifers ahead to enter Shiplake Copse in a corner of the field. Inside this wood, bear half right and follow a path along the inside edge of the wood then beside a left-hand boundary bank. On leaving the wood, follow its outside edge, later a left-hand hedge straight on through two fields to reach the Binfield Heath road.

Turn left onto this road and just beyond a left-hand bend, turn right into Green Lane (path ED5) and follow it to its far end. Here, by a garage, turn left onto a path through a belt of trees which then continues between garden fences to Gravel Road. Turn left onto this road, then turn right through the second gap in the hedge (still on path ED5) following a crop break to the end of a hedge. Here go past the end of the hedge then bear right following a right-hand hedge which turns left at one point. Just before a kink in the hedge, turn right through a gap in it, then turn left following its other side soon entering a fenced path. On reaching a green lane called Taggs Lane (bridleway ED18), turn left into it and follow its winding course for nearly half a mile, ignoring a crossing path and a drive to the right, then along a macadamed lane to reach Dunsden Green.

Here turn left onto a road and at a road junction by the old village well, which was dug in 1878 and is 150 feet deep, turn right onto the Reading road. Soon after the left-hand houses end, turn left over a stile onto path ED11, following the right-hand side of the hedge ahead with views across Reading to your right. Where three hedges meet, go straight on through a hedge gap, then bear left, following a left-hand hedge to several trees in it. By an oak tree, turn right across the field following what is normally a crop break, with panoramic views of the Thames Valley opening up ahead and to left and right, finally dropping down to a stile and flight of steps right of the garage of a long thatched cottage called 'Botany Bay'. Descend the steps and cross the A4155 carefully, then turn left along its narrow verge and follow it to the 'Flowing Spring'. Just past the pub, turn right into Flowing Spring Lane and follow it past the pub car park and over a bridge. At a right-hand bend, cross a stile in the left-hand hedge and take path ED12 following the back of the roadside hedge through two fields. At the far end of the second field, cross a stile to rejoin Flowing Spring Lane, then follow it straight on to its junction with the B478. Cross this busy road carefully and take bridleway ED21 straight on through a bridlegate onto the old line of the road which leads you back to your starting point.

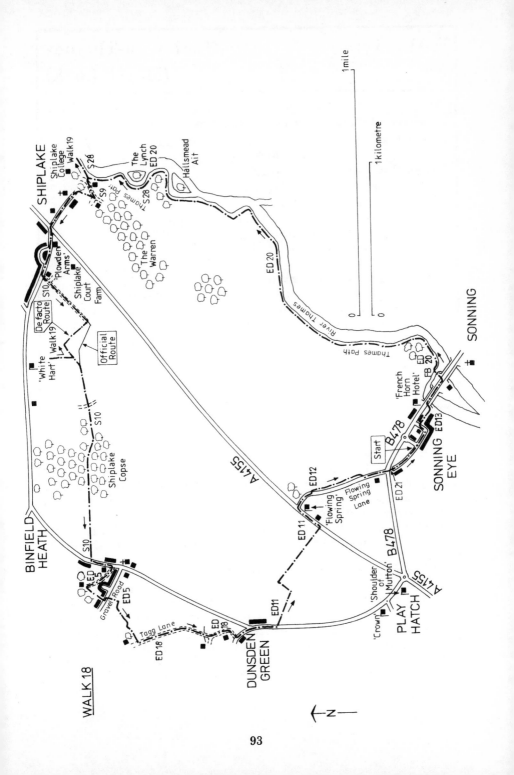

WALK 18

93

WALK 19: Henley-on-Thames (Marsh Lock)

Length of Walk: 7.6 miles / 12.2 Km

Starting Point: Entrance to Mill Lane car park, near Marsh Lock.

Grid Ref: SU771817

Maps: OS Landranger Sheet 175
OS Explorer Sheet 171
OS Pathfinder Sheets 1156 (SU68/78)
(or old Explorer Sheet 3) & 1172 (SU67/77)
Chiltern Society FP Map No. 4 &
East Berks RA Group FP Map No. 5

How to get there / Parking: Mill Lane car park, 0.8 miles south-east of the centre of Henley-on-Thames, may be reached from the town centre by taking the A4155 towards Reading. On the outskirts of Henley, just past the 'Jolly Waterman', turn left into Mill Lane (signposted to the Sports Centre) and follow the road over a railway bridge to a car park on the left-hand side.

Marsh Lock, where the towpath traverses the weir stream by long wooden bridges above and below the weir, is one of the most picturesque locks on the River Thames. This is due both to the steep wooded backcloth of Remenham Hill and the immaculately-kept grounds of riverside properties on the Berkshire bank, as well as the natural beauty of the expanse of riverside meadows on the Oxfordshire bank south of the lock.

Although the walk does not start at the lock itself, you return by way of the towpath through these lush meadows and over the bridges to the lock. Before that, however, this walk, which combines attractive wooded hill country with the unique beauty of the River Thames, also takes you by way of Harpsden in its secluded valley onto a plateau at Upper Bolney and explores various parts of the scattered village of Shiplake, including its church and lock.

Starting from the entrance to the car park in Mill Lane, turn right along this road, crossing the railway bridge and returning to the A4155. Cross this and go straight on along Waterman's Road. Where the road turns right, leave it and take bridleway H20 straight on, passing between concrete posts. On reaching a road junction, take Peppard Lane, a narrow macadam road, straight on uphill for a third of a mile. The name Peppard Lane is interesting as it is a surviving reminder of the ancient 'strip-parish' system which can be found all along the Chiltern escarpment and its Thames frontage, whereby both upland and lowland villages were allocated a narrow strip of land stretching from the lowland plain or the riverside up into the hills, each of which normally had a spine road to connect its various parts. Rotherfield Peppard, after which this road is named, was, indeed, just such a parish extending for five miles from the river at Marsh Lock to the Chiltern watershed west of the mother village and Peppard Lane was part of its spine road. About 75 yards beyond its junction with Berkshire Road, turn left into fenced path H2, which is partially blocked by a tubular steel safety rail. Follow this path straight on, soon crossing the end of a residential road and continuing to reach a stile into a field with a fine view of Harpsden Bottom ahead. Now follow a right-hand fence straight on downhill to a stile into fenced path HA20 which leads you out to the village street in Harpsden.

Harpsden is a rather unusual village in that it consists of several small hamlets spaced at intervals along the road in the valley bottom. The hamlet which you are now visiting appears to be the most populous and contains the Victorian village school and the village hall, but the original village with its twelfth-century parish church and the manor house known as Harpsden Court, part of which dates from the thirteenth century, is half a mile to the east.

Turn right along the village street past the school and village hall, then, at a road junction, turn left onto the road signposted to Binfield Heath and Reading. After about 80 yards, just past a clump of tall trees and a raised golf tee, turn left onto path HA23 up a flight of steps and through a copse onto the golf course. Now turn right along a route marked by yellow posts across a fairway, looking out for balls being driven from your right, to reach a corner of Harpsden Wood, then follow a stony track uphill. Near the top, bear slightly left, passing just left of a tee, skirting a copse and keeping just left of two small bunkers to cross a stile. Now follow a left-hand fence straight on through two paddocks and a large field to reach a stile in the left-hand fence. Do not cross this, but turn right onto path HA6, following a left-hand hedge to a stile into a lane at Upper Bolney. Turn right into this lane and fork immediately left onto a track towards a cottage. On reaching the edge of High Wood, ignore a crossing track and take a track (still HA6) straight on into the wood. Just inside the wood, fork left and follow a waymarked track through it to a stile into a field. Now take path S14 straight on across the field to cross a stile into a plantation. In the plantation, follow an obvious path straight on downhill to cross a stile into a field. Now go straight on, joining a left-hand hedge and following its winding course uphill to a hedge gap into the next field. Here bear half right across the field to a stile to the left of two modern houses. Cross this and follow an alleyway between gardens out to Kiln Lane at Binfield Heath.

Turn left onto this rough road (S32) and follow it for over half a mile, leaving Binfield Heath and passing through Long Copse. By a large part-brick, part-wooden bungalow on the left, turn right through a gap in the hedge onto path S33 and follow a right-hand hedge to a gate leading out onto a road. Cross the road and go through a gap in the left-hand hedge of the 'White Hart' car park onto path S11. Now follow the pub's boundary fence to the rear corner of its garden, then bear half left across the field, heading for a double-posted electricity pylon by the corner of a clump of bushes. At this point, at the time of writing, it is necessary to take a *de facto* path which is subject to alteration. Walkers are advised to heed any signs or waymarks. Here turn sharp left onto the *de facto* route of path S10 (joining the reverse direction of Walk 18), following a crop break to the corner of a fence, then turning right and following a left-hand fence to a stile in it where you rejoin the official path. Turn left over this stile and follow a grassy track for a quarter mile, joining a concrete road and continuing straight on to a road at Shiplake. Here turn right and follow the road to the A4155 at the 'Plowden Arms' crossroads. Cross the main road and continue straight on up Church Lane to Shiplake Church (described in the text of Walk 18).

At the end of the lane by the church, go through a gate and bear half right down a narrow enclosed bridleway (S9). On emerging at a crossways, turn left onto a wider track and follow it to reach the river. At the river bank, leave the track and turn left onto the Thames towpath (S28), parting company again with Walk 18, joining the Thames Path and following the river for two-thirds of a mile to Shiplake Lock. Here cross a stile and turn left onto a fenced path beside a wall leading to Mill Lane. Turn right onto this road, then, after a few yards, turn left through a gap by an old stile onto fenced path S2. Cross a further stile, then follow a left-hand fence straight on to a stile under a lime tree. Bear half left over this stile and make for a further stile leading to a raised road. Turn left onto this road subsequently crossing a bridge. At a road junction, turn right into Mill Road and follow it for nearly half a mile to the 'Baskerville Arms' crossroads at Lower Shiplake.

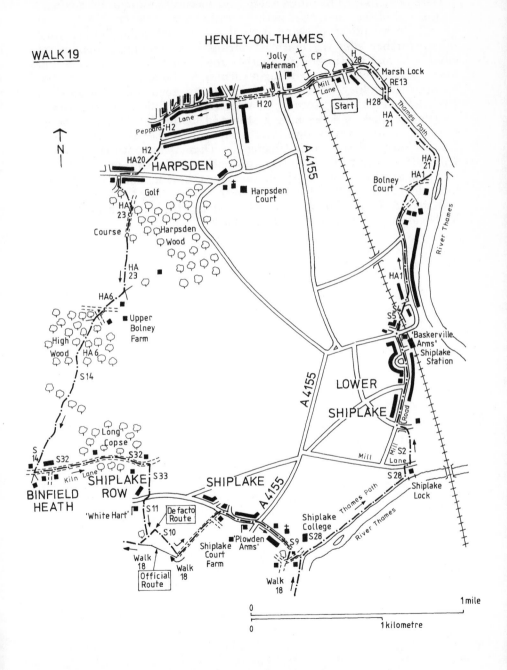

Here bear half right into a cul-de-sac, passing Shiplake Post Office. At the end of the road, take path S5 straight on between a hedge and a fence to a railway crossing with stiles on each side. Beyond this, take a further alleyway (path S4) straight on, crossing a residential cul-de-sac and continuing to another road. Turn left along this and follow it to its end, disregarding a turning to the left and passing the entrance to Bolney Court. At the end of the road, take fenced path HA1 left of the entrance to 'Fairacres' and follow it, eventually crossing a track and reaching a stile and footbridge. Having crossed these, continue straight on to the river bank at the site of the former Bolney Ferry. Now turn left along the Thames towpath (HA21) and follow this beautiful section of towpath to Marsh Lock. Here go through a gate (now on H28), then over a long footbridge to the lockside (briefly on RE13) and back over another long footbridge to the Oxfordshire bank. On reaching this, leaving the Thames Path, take Mill Lane straight on back to the car park.

WALK 20:   Henley-on-Thames

Length of Walk: (A) 8.3 miles / 13.3 Km
                     (B) 7.2 miles / 11.6 Km

Starting Point: Telephone box at junction of Badgemore Lane
                     and Luker Avenue, Henley-on-Thames.

Grid Ref: SU758830

Maps: OS Landranger Sheet 175
           OS Explorer Sheet 171 (or old Sheet 3)
           OS Pathfinder Sheet 1156 (SU68/78)
           Chiltern Society FP Maps Nos. 2 & 11

How to get there / Parking: Due to lack of medium- or
long-term parking spaces in car parks on the north side of
Henley-on-Thames, it is necessary to start this walk in the
suburbs where unrestricted on-street parking is possible.
From Henley town centre take the A4130 towards Oxford.
About 50 yards beyond the roundabout where the A4155
forks off to the right towards Marlow, turn left into
Badgemore Lane. At a T-junction, turn right into Luker
Avenue and find a suitable parking space in this or a
branching road.

Henley-on-Thames, home of the famous Royal Regatta, has, for
the last century or more, been a fashionable riverside resort.
Although this has, to some extent, contributed to the
architectural beauty of the town, its former role as a
commercial centre is responsible for much of its legacy of
picturesque buildings. Prior to the age of railways, the town
was of commercial importance, being both a river port and a
bridgehead on a main road crossing the Thames. In Hart
Street, the street leading from the bridge to Henley Town Hall,
are to be found a number of ancient timber-framed houses and
inns, some dating back to the fifteenth and sixteenth
centuries. The Town Hall around which the street divides, was
built in 1796 on the site of the mediaeval Guildhall and the
imposing Parish Church by the bridge and nearby almshouses
date from the fourteenth to sixteenth centuries. Henley
Bridge, surely one of the most graceful on the Thames, was
built in 1786 to replace a wooden structure swept away by a
flood in 1774.

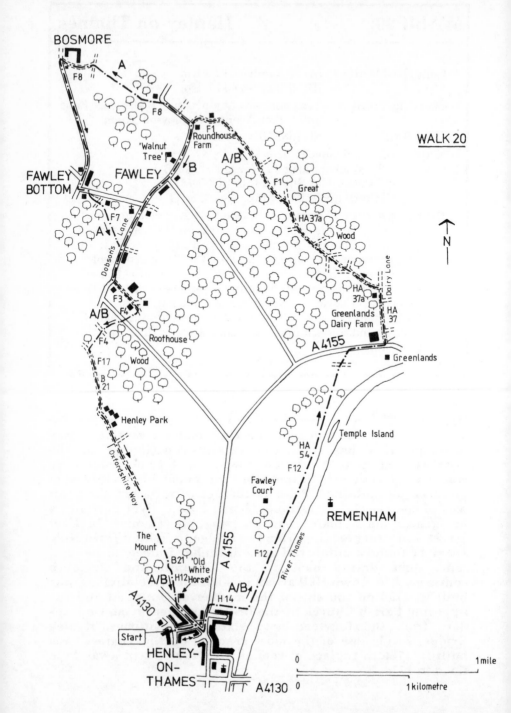

BOSMORE

F8

A

F8

'Walnut Tree'

F1
Roundhouse Farm

B

A/B

F1

Great

HA 37a

Wood

FAWLEY BOTTOM

FAWLEY

F7

A

Dobson's Lane

F3

F4

A/B

F4

F17

Wood

B 21

Roothouse

Henley Park

Oxfordshire Way

The Mount

B21 'Old White Horse'

A/B

H12

A/B

H 14

A4130

Start

HENLEY-ON-THAMES

A4130

HA 37a

Dairy Lane

HA 37

Greenlands Dairy Farm

A 4155

Greenlands

Temple Island

HA 54

F12

Fawley Court

REMENHAM

F12

River Thames

A 4155

WALK 20

N

0   1 mile

0   1 kilometre

100

The walk first leads you to the river and follows the Regatta course past Fawley Court and Temple Island to Greenlands, then climbs through woodlands to the remote heights of Fawley. Here you can either take a scenic extension via Bosmore and Fawley Bottom or follow the road through the village before returning by way of the commanding Henley Park ridge to Henley-on-Thames.

Starting from the telephone box at the junction of Badgemore Lane and Luker Avenue, take Badgemore Lane to the A4130, then turn right to reach the roundabout at its junction with the A4155. Here turn left onto the A4155 towards Marlow. After passing the drive to Phyllis Court, at a slight right-hand bend, turn right through the frame of an old kissing-gate beside a larger gate onto path H14 and follow it beside a right-hand fence to a kissing-gate near the river. Go through this, then turn left along the river bank. Now take path H14 (later F12, then HA54) following the Thames closely for more than a mile. After just over half a mile, Fawley Court, a mansion built for William Freeman to a design by Sir Christopher Wren in the 1680s and now a Polish school known as the College of Divine Mercy, can be seen to the left from one of the many footbridges on this path. To the right at the same point on the other side of the river is the picturesque village of Remenham. Further on is Temple Island, so named because of the small temple designed by Wyatt on its southern tip which is nowadays the starting point of the Regatta course.

Near the far end of the island, path HA54 begins to bear away from the river and crosses two footbridges in a belt of trees. Here go straight on across the next field to a further footbridge, then continue straight on crossing the macadam drive to Greenlands, a large Victorian mansion to your right built by the famous bookseller W H Smith in 1871 and now a management college. 150 yards further on, a stile leads you out onto the A4155. Turn right along this road and where its pavement ends, cross the road carefully and take bridleway HA37 through a fence gap opposite, soon joining a farm road and passing the former Greenlands Dairy Farm. Follow this farm road for a quarter mile, then, by a metal gate just past some red-brick cottages, turn left onto bridleway HA37a, a fenced track. Where it opens out into a field, bear half right, climbing to the edge of Great Wood. Here turn round for a fine view down the Thames Valley towards Bisham Hill before entering the wood. In the wood, disregard all branching and crossing tracks or paths and follow a waymarked track straight on through it. After about a quarter mile you pass through an old gateway and after a further quarter mile, the waymarked track twists to the left and becomes bridleway F1. You then resume your previous direction and continue for a further third of a mile, finally emerging from Great Wood. Now go straight on along a lane between a fence and a hedge with fine views to the south, eventually reaching a road at Fawley by Roundhouse Farm which is believed originally to have been a windmill. Here, if wishing to take **Walk A**, omit the next paragraph.

Walk B now turns left onto the road and follows it through the scattered village of Fawley for a mile, passing the 'Walnut Tree', a road to the left, a road to the right and Fawley Church hidden in trees. This twelfth-century church with a later tower and a chancel rebuilt in Italian style in 1748 contains some ornate Jacobean woodwork as well as a marble monument with alabaster effigies of Sir James Whitelocke and his wife, parents of the judge who refused to pass judgement on Charles I. In the churchyard there are also two large mausoleums containing the remains of the Freeman and Mackenzie families who, for centuries, owned Fawley Court. Now continue along the road for a further 700 yards and omit the next paragraph.

By Roundhouse Farm, **Walk A** turns right onto the road and follows it for some 250 yards. Just before a sharp right-hand bend by a cottage, turn left through a hedge gap onto path F8 and follow it between hedges and fences, into a belt of scrub. Now go straight on downhill passing through a strip of woodland and emerging into a field. Here follow a powerline straight on uphill to a junction of tracks by the corner of a hedge. Take a track straight on beside the hedge to reach Bosmore Farm. Now follow the track straight on, bearing slightly right at one point, then pass left of most of the farm buildings to reach a road. Turn left onto this road and follow it for two-thirds of a mile descending gently into Fawley Bottom. Here, at the first road junction go straight on, then, at the second road junction turn left onto the road signposted to Fawley and follow it steeply uphill into a wood. After about 100 yards, fork right over a stile by a gate onto path F7. After a few yards, keep right at a fork and follow the waymarked path straight on, ignoring a crossing path and emerging through a kissing-gate into a field. Now bear half right across the field, passing right of a telegraph pole to reach a stile. Cross this and bear half left, heading towards a house with a steep roof and broad chimney stack to reach gates leading to the ridgetop road through Fawley. Turn right onto this and follow it for about 300 yards.

At a sharp right-hand bend, where a chestnut tree, a fire hydrant and a footpath sign are clustered together on a triangle of grass to the left, **Walks A and B** turn left into a rough lane (path F3). After some 350 yards, just past the gates to Homer House, turn right onto path F4, following a right-hand hedge, passing right of a barn and continuing between fences to a corner of Roothouse Wood. Here ignore a track forking left into the wood and continue straight on downhill between fences to a road. Cross this road, bear slightly right over a stile and follow the outside edge of the wood crossing two more stiles. Now cross the drive to an underground reservoir and continue straight on over a stile opposite. On reaching a field, follow its right-hand hedge straight on to enter a stony lane (path F17 and part of the Oxfordshire Way). Turn left here and follow the lane for half a mile, becoming path B21 and passing Henley Park House. Where the lane (now a macadam private road) turns sharp left, take path B21 straight on through a kissing-gate by double gates and follow a farm track straight on to reach a farm shed. Here go through another kissing-gate and continue straight on across open parkland on the top of what is known as The Mount until you eventually drop down to a kissing-gate into a wood. Now follow an obvious path downhill through the wood. On leaving the wood, the path (now H12) becomes enclosed between a hedge and a fence and continues to the A4130. Turn left along this, then, after 300 yards, turn right into Badgemore Lane for your point of departure.

WALK 21: Lower Assendon

Length of Walk: 5.5 miles / 8.8 Km

Starting Point: Junction of A4130 and B480 (Assendons/Stonor road) at the Lower Assendon end of the Henley Fairmile.

Grid Ref: SU746845

Maps: OS Landranger Sheet 175
OS Explorer Sheet 171 (or old Sheet 3)
OS Pathfinder Sheet 1156 (SU68/78)
Chiltern Society FP Map No. 2

How to get there / Parking: Lower Assendon, 1.6 miles northwest of Henley-on-Thames, may be reached from the town by taking the A4130 towards Oxford for 1.5 miles. At the far end of a long straight known as The Fairmile, turn right onto the Assendons and Stonor road, then, after about 50 yards, park in a layby on the right by the village telephone box.

Lower Assendon, at the opposite end of The Fairmile from its famous neighbour Henley-on-Thames, is today a small sleepy village clustered around the junctions of a 'B' road and two minor roads, but its old coaching inn, the 'Golden Ball', betrays its former role as a crossroads between the eighteenth-century route of the Henley – Oxford turnpike road via Old Bix Hill, the more ancient route of this road via Bix Bottom and the minor road to Fawley. It was only in around 1800 when the present less steep and tortuous route of the A4130 was constructed that the village lost this pivotal position.

The walk indeed commences by following the old route of the turnpike road for a short distance before crossing the modern A4130 and climbing to the wooded heights of Lambridge Wood. It then continues by way of the secluded historic mansion of Greys Court with its castle ruins and more woodland to the picturesque village of Greys Green which, in Spring, is a mass of cherry blossom. The return is by way of a more open route via Rotherfield Greys with its interesting church and Lambridge Wood before dropping with a fine view to the north to reach Lower Assendon.

Starting from the junction of the A4130 and B480 (Assendons and Stonor road) at the end of The Fairmile just outside Lower Assendon, take the B480 into Lower Assendon. After about 150 yards by the aptly-named Flint Cottage, fork left into a narrow lane which is Old Bix Hill and the eighteenth-century line of the turnpike road. Follow this past a number of cottages and rounding a left-hand then a right-hand bend. Now about 40 yards beyond a speed delimiting sign, turn left onto a path through a hedge gap to reach the A4130. Cross this dual-carriageway at the point where there is a gap in the hedge on its central reservation and then turn right along its verge. After a few yards, turn left through a green gate onto path B24, then turn immediately left through a second gate and turn right to follow a right-hand hedge uphill. Where the hedge begins to bear left, go straight on through it and follow a path uphill through scrubland to a rail-stile. Cross this and go straight on uphill to a kissing-gate into a field. Now go straight on uphill passing between a cattle trough and an electricity pole then through a kissing-gate to enter Lambridge Wood. Inside the wood, take path RG27, joining a gravel drive and following it straight on, soon bearing right and joining bridleway RG29. At a second right-hand bend, leave the drive and take waymarked path RG11 straight on into the woods. Follow this winding waymarked path straight on through the woods for two-thirds of a mile, ignoring all crossing or branching tracks or paths, until you reach a road at the hamlet of Broadplat.

Turn left onto this road, then turn immediately right opposite a cottage onto the macadam drive to 'Forge Works' (path RG11). Where the drive forks, go left, then turn immediately left again onto fenced path RG7 along the edge of a field. Go past the works and a barn, then turn left over a stile by a gate. Here turn right and take a grassy track straight on, ignoring a branching path to the right, using a wooden floodwalk to pass a pond and crossing a stile by a gate. Now follow a right-hand hedge straight on through two fields, with Greys Court coming into view to your right in the second field, to reach a macadam drive by the National Trust information office.

Greys Court has had a chequered history. The mediaeval castle, built by the de Grey family from which the name 'Greys' is derived, was fortified by the construction of a surrounding wall in 1348. Four of the five towers and part of the wall still survive. The stables and a donkey-wheel well-house remain from an Elizabethan house built by the Knollys family which was destroyed in the Civil War, but the house which stands here today is of late Stuart origin and in design resembles many large Oxfordshire houses.

By the information office, turn right onto the drive which is still path RG7 (the use of which requires no payment unless you deviate to visit the house) and follow it straight on, with a good view of the house to your right at one point, ignoring three branches to your right. Where the drive turns left, leave it and go straight on across the grass to a stile in bushes leading to Rocky Lane. Cross this road and a stile opposite onto path RG6, going straight on downhill and up again to a stile into a wood. Continue straight on uphill through the wood, crossing two further stiles, then follow a left-hand hedge straight on to reach the cricket green at Greys Green.

Here bear right around the edge of the green to reach a road junction at its far corner, then turn right onto the major road. Where this road forks, keep left, going through a copse. At the far end of the copse, turn left through gates onto fenced bridleway RG14 and follow this straight on for over half a mile, rounding a left-hand bend at one point with Rotherfield Greys Church coming into view to your left. Where the bridleway (now P18) turns right and becomes enclosed between hedges, continue to follow it for a further 150 yards, looking out for a slightly concealed stile in the left-hand hedge. Turn left over this onto path RG15 and go straight across the field to a stile left of a holly tree. Now head for Rotherfield Greys Church to cross a further stile leading to a path alongside the churchyard wall which brings you out to a road in Rotherfield Greys near the 'Maltsters Arms'.

The Church of St. Nicholas, built by the de Grey family in the thirteenth century, is noteworthy for a fine brass of Robert de Grey (d. 1387) in the chancel and the burial chapel of the Knollys family with its colourful tomb and monuments, added in 1605.

Turn right onto the road passing the church, then turn left through a kissing-gate opposite a telephone box onto path RG16 along an avenue of trees. At the far end of this avenue, join a right-hand fence and follow it descending gradually to a stile, then follow a left-hand hedge to a gap leading you down to a stile. Cross this and turn right onto path RG17. On reaching a gate and stile, do not cross these, but turn left onto path RG18, following a right-hand fence uphill to a rail stile in the fence just short of a belt of trees. Cross this stile and continue up the right-hand side of the tree-belt to reach gates and rails leading to a crossing farm track. Turn right onto this track, swinging left, joining a concrete farm road and following it straight on to reach a road. Turn right along its verge, then, after about 80 yards, turn left crossing the road and a stile by a gate onto path RG27 following a left-hand fence. At the far end of the field, cross a stile right of a gate and bear slightly right across the next field to join the right-hand edge of a belt of trees, then follow it to a stile into Lambridge Wood. Cross this and turn right onto path RG25, dropping into the bottom of a dip. Here turn sharp left onto path RG28 into a plantation and soon disregard a crossing track. On emerging into

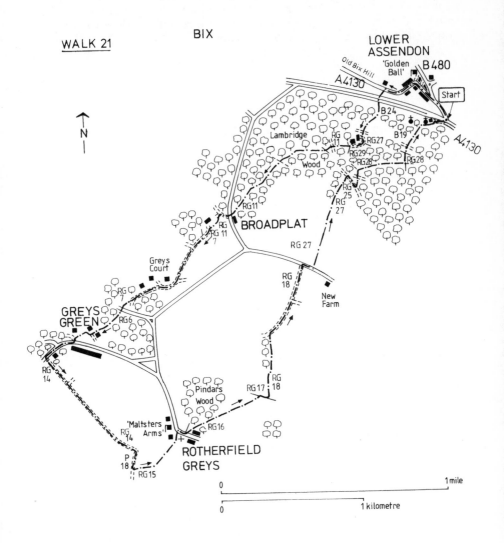

WALK 21

BIX

LOWER ASSENDON

Old Bix Hill

'Golden Ball'

B480

A4130

Start

B24

A4130

Lambridge

RG 11

RG27

B19

RG29

RG26

RG28

Wood

RG 25

RG 27

RG11

BROADPLAT

RG 11 7

RG 27

Greys Court

RG 18

New Farm

RG 7

GREYS GREEN

RG6

RG 14

RG 18

Pindars Wood

RG 17

RG 18

'Maltsters Arms'

RG 16

RG 14

ROTHERFIELD GREYS

P 18

RG 15

↑ N

0 — 1 mile

0 — 1 kilometre

mature beechwoods, turn right and follow the edge of the plantation, later with a younger plantation to your left. At the far end of the younger plantation, take a waymarked path going left at a fork into mature woodland to reach a crossways. Here take fenced bridleway B19 straight on out of the wood, crossing a macadam drive with a superb view of the Assendon Valley ahead and dropping downhill for some 350 yards to emerge by the gates of a cemetery, then turn right onto its drive to reach your starting point.

WALK 22: Middle Assendon

Length of Walk: 6.0 miles / 9.6 Km
Starting Point: 'Rainbow', Middle Assendon.
Grid Ref: SU739858
Maps: OS Landranger Sheet 175
OS Explorer Sheet 171 (or old Sheet 3)
OS Pathfinder Sheet 1156 (SU68/78)
Chiltern Society FP Map No. 2

How to get there / Parking: Middle Assendon, 2.5 miles northwest of Henley-on-Thames, may be reached from the town by taking the A4130 towards Oxford for 1.5 miles. At the far end of a long straight known as The Fairmile, turn right onto the Assendons and Stonor road and follow it for about a mile to Middle Assendon where you can park in a long parking bay on the left-hand side, taking care not to obstruct the entrances to any drives.

Notes: Heavy nettle growth may be encountered at several points in the summer months.

Middle Assendon, situated at the point where a number of roads converge and notably where the ancient Oxford road through Bix Bottom and the modern B480 part company, was originally, as its name suggests, the middle village of three bearing the name 'Assendon'. In 1896, however, as part of the major reform of local government, Upper Assendon, which had formerly been a detached manor of the parish of Pyrton, became an independent parish and was renamed Stonor after the nearby manor house and its family and so only Lower and Middle Assendon now remain, but the name Upper Assendon survives as the name of a seventeenth-century farm in the village.

The walk, which must be one of the scenically most beautiful in the whole of the Chilterns, starts from Middle Assendon's picturesque village inn, the 'Rainbow', and first leads you up to Bix's airy hilltop common before continuing through woodland to drop with superb views into Bix Bottom. After climbing to Maidensgrove, more spectacular views are encountered on your descent towards Stonor, but having made a further steep climb to Coxlease Farm, the walk culminates

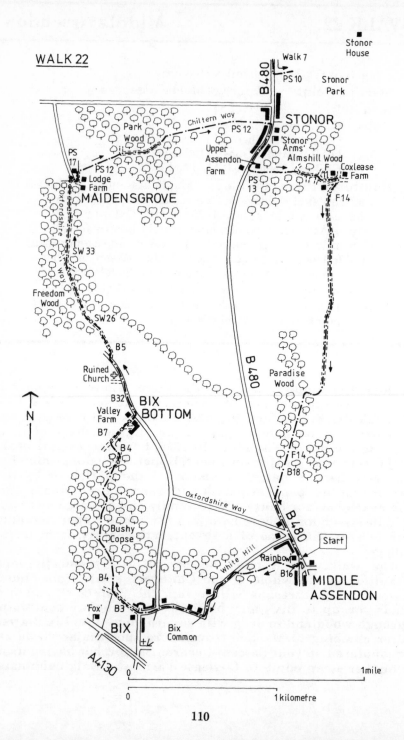

by following a ridgetop track with breathtaking views across the hills and valleys to the west and south before dropping back into Middle Assendon.

Starting from the 'Rainbow' in Middle Assendon, take the B480 towards Henley for a few yards, then, by a telephone box, turn right onto path B16, a grassy track leading to a gate and stile. Cross the stile and bear slightly right across a field with a fine view down the valley to your left to cross a stile in the far corner. Now follow a fenced path uphill to another stile, then continue up an avenue of conifers to a stile by gates which leads you in a few yards to a narrow road called White Hill, presumably because it once had a chalky surface. Turn left onto this road and follow it uphill with brief glimpses of Bix Bottom through the hedge to your right and towards Henley through the hedge to your left. On reaching Bix Common at the top of the hill, continue to follow the road along its edge with Bix Church coming into view to your left. This church was built in 1874 to replace one in Bix Bottom which is now in ruins and is thought to be a consequence of the village having 'migrated' from the route of the ancient Oxford road through Bix Bottom to the modern route through Bix. However it is also believed that there were originally two separate villages, each with its own church, but no trace remains of the original mediaeval church in Bix which was then known as 'Bixgwybynt'.

At a road junction, go straight on, then, at a sharp left-hand bend, leave the road and take bridleway B3, a gravel lane, straight on, soon entering an open field and continuing along a grassy track. After about 170 yards, by a cattle trough to your left, turn right onto an ill-defined crossing path (B4) and head for a stile into a wood called Bushy Copse. Cross this and follow a waymarked path along the inside edge of the wood. After about 200 yards, ignore a branching path to your left and go deeper into the wood, soon with a fine view ahead across the Bix and Assendon bottoms. On reaching the corner of a field to your right, continue along the inside edge of the wood, eventually joining a track and reaching a gate overlooking Valley Farm. Do not go through this gate but turn left, following a right-hand fence to a stile into a field, then continue to follow the fence downhill to a gate and stile in the valley bottom. Cross this stile and turn right onto path B7, a farm track, and follow it to a gate into Valley Farm. Go through this, then, where the track turns right into the farmyard, leave it and go straight on through a five-bar-gate and past a farmhouse and other farm buildings to reach Bix Bottom Lane (B32). Turn left onto this ancient road to Oxford and follow it for a quarter mile passing the ruins of the Norman church which closed when the present church at Bix was completed. This marks the site of the lost village of Bixbrand which is shown on old maps and can be detected in aerial photographs.

About 100 yards beyond the ruined church, turn right into a hedged lane (bridleway B5 and part of the Oxfordshire Way and Oxfordshire Cycle Way) and follow this uphill into Freedom Wood. Here follow the obvious track (now bridleway SW26) straight on uphill through the wood for just over a quarter mile. On reaching a track junction with a field visible through the hedge ahead, bear slightly left joining Warmscombe Lane (SW33) and follow this ancient cart track straight on for a third of a mile to reach the end of a macadam road at Maidensgrove. Here, joining the Chiltern Way, turn sharp right onto the road into Lodge Farm, then, just before entering the farmyard, turn left onto a hedged track (bridleway PS17) which leads you into a field. On entering the field, fork half right onto path PS12 (leaving the Oxfordshire Way) and head for a stile on the edge of Park Wood. Just inside the wood, join a track and follow its waymarked course straight on. Eventually the track narrows to a path and goes straight on to reach a stile where a superb view opens out towards Stonor Park and village. Cross this stile and go straight on downhill, passing just left of two copses to reach a stile in a sporadic hedge. Here go straight on, passing just right of a telegraph pole to cross a stile under a yew tree at the edge of the village. Now continue between garden hedges to the B480.

Leaving the Chiltern Way, turn right along the narrow nearside verge and follow it through this picturesque village passing the 'Stonor Arms' and Upper Assendon Farm. At the far end of the farm buildings, cross the road and a stile opposite and take path PS13 following a left-hand fence uphill to a stile into Almshill Wood. Turn round for a last look across the roofs of the village, then cross the stile and follow an obvious path straight on uphill. Near the top, ignore a branching track to the left, then soon join a flint track at a bend and follow it straight on uphill. At a crossways, bear slightly right onto a track beside a left-hand hedge (path F11) and follow this uphill to Coxlease Farm. Go past two left-hand barns and a well-kept cypress hedge, then turn right through double gates to a track junction. Here take the central option (path F14), bearing half right and following its fenced course past the farmhouse, then bearing left. Now continue straight on along the ridgetop for three-quarters of a mile with panoramic views ahead and to your right. Where the track ends, bear right following a right-hand hedge dropping down to a stile into Paradise Wood. In the wood the path swings to the left and follows its top edge for a third of a mile until you leave the wood with Middle Assendon coming into view ahead. Here bear half right onto path B18 descending across a field to a hedge gap onto the B480 by a small concrete gas installation. Turn left onto this road and follow it back into Middle Assendon.

WALK 23:   Hambleden (North)

Length of Walk: 6.0 miles / 9.7 Km

Starting Point: Entrance to public car park near the
'Stag & Huntsman', Hambleden.

Grid Ref: SU785866

Maps: OS Landranger Sheet 175
OS Explorer Sheet 171 (or old Sheet 3)
OS Pathfinder Sheet 1156 (SU68/78)
Chiltern Society FP Map No. 11

How to get there / Parking: Hambleden, 4 miles west of
Marlow, may be reached from the town by taking the
winding A4155 towards Henley-on-Thames for 4.5 miles
to Mill End, then turning right onto a road signposted to
Hambleden, Skirmett and Fingest. After nearly a mile
fork right onto a road signposted to the village centre,
then just past the church, leave the major road and go
straight on past the 'Stag and Huntsman' to a public car
park on the right.

Hambleden, set in its beautiful valley flanked by beechwoods,
remains an unspoilt Chiltern village thanks to the Hambleden
Estate which owns much of it and the National Trust, to which
most of it is covenanted. This has both largely saved the
village from modern development and made it the ideal setting
for a number of historical films. Around the village square
with its pump and along narrow lanes leading off it are a
number of attractive cottages and old-world shops, mostly in
characteristic Chiltern brick-and-flint, as well as the village
pub, the Jacobean manor house and the parish church. Built
in the fourteenth century, the church was given its present
tower in 1721 which was heightened in 1883 when extensive
renovations took place. Despite this, it has retained several
fine monuments and in its churchyard is the grave of the
Victorian bookseller and government minister, W. H. Smith,
whose descendants still live in the manor house. This house
was also the birthplace of Lord Cardigan, who led the Charge
of the Light Brigade in the Crimean War, while another
famous son of the village was St. Thomas de Cantelupe, a
thirteenth-century Bishop of Hereford and advisor of Edward I,

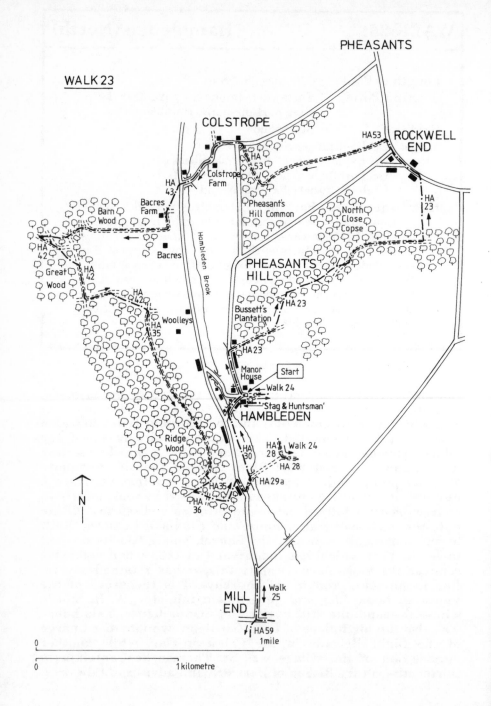

WALK 23

PHEASANTS

COLSTROPE

HA53 ROCKWELL END

HA 53

Colstrope Farm

HA 43

Bacres Farm

Barn Wood

HA 42

Bacres

Great Wood

HA 42

HA 42

HA 35

Woolleys

Pheasant's Hill Common

North Close Copse

HA 23

Hambleden Brook

PHEASANT'S HILL

HA 23

Bussett's Plantation

HA 23

Manor House

Start

Walk 24

'Stag & Huntsman'

HAMBLEDEN

N

Ridge Wood

HA 30

HA 28

Walk 24

HA 28

HA 35

HA 29a

HA 36

MILL END

Walk 25

HA 59

0   1 mile

0   1 kilometre

114

who was canonised in 1320 following a series of miracles which took place at his tomb in Hereford Cathedral.

The walk explores the wooded hills on either side of the valley, first climbing to the hilltop plateau to the east and the hamlet of Rockwell End before crossing the valley at Colstrope to the wooded hills on its western side. Despite the fact that considerable lengths of the walk are within woodland, this does not prevent it also being characterised by fine views along and across both the Hambleden and Thames valleys.

Starting from the entrance to Hambleden public car park, turn left down the lane past the 'Stag and Huntsman'. At a road junction by the church, turn right passing the church to your left and the manor house to your right. On rounding a bend, turn right by a yew tree onto path HA23, a stony lane between cottages, and follow it uphill entering a wood called Bussett's Plantation. Just before leaving the wood, ignore a stile into woodland to your left, then some 30 yards further on, opposite a gate, turn left up a bank and over a stile. Now bear half right over the hill to reach a stile into further woodland. At the top of the rise, stop to admire views ahead across the hills towards Stokenchurch (marked by the BT tower) and behind across the Thames Valley to Remenham Hill. Just inside the wood, where the village of Pheasant's Hill comes into view in the valley below, turn right onto a path (still HA23) following a left-hand fence along the top edge of the wood. Where the top edge of the wood turns right away from the path, ignore a crossing path and continue straight on. At a second junction at the edge of mature woodland, disregard a crossing track and keep straight on joining another track. After some 350 yards the path enters a neck of woodland which later leads into a copse. Here turn left through a gap (still on path HA23) and go straight across a large field to a stile just right of a farm and clump of trees at Rockwell End.

Cross this stile and turn left onto a road through this hamlet named after the Rocolte or Rockholl family who are recorded as farming in the area at various dates from the fourteenth to seventeenth centuries. At a fork in the road, bear right and at a second road junction, go straight on, then at a right-hand bend, turn left onto path HA53, a rough track with fine views opening out across the Hambleden and Thames valleys. Eventually you enter a hedged lane which leads you into a wood called Pheasant's Hill Common where there is an abundance of ancient Chiltern yew trees. On rounding a sharp bend, ignore a crossing path and continue straight on, descending gradually to reach a road near Colstrope.

Here disregard a rough track to your left and turn left onto the macadam road. Follow this downhill through the hamlet of Colstrope, passing the traditional Chiltern brick-and-flint Colstrope Farm, crossing a bridge over Hambleden Brook and reaching the valley spine road. Here bear half left crossing the road and passing through a hedge gap onto path HA43. Now bear half left towards outbuildings at Bacres Farm to reach a gate. This farm was originally named Baker's Farm after the Baker family who farmed it, but after it was sold to W. H. Smith in 1866, for some reason the spelling was altered to the unusual form in use today.

Go through the gate, then bear half left again onto a farm road passing left of the farm. Where this road turns right, follow it climbing steeply and eventually entering Barn Wood. Near the top of the hill, where the track forks, bear left, then ignore a crossing track. By the corner of a field to your left, at a series of three forks, go left, then right, then left again and take a winding waymarked path straight on into a plantation. Ignore the first crossing track and on reaching a second (path HA42), turn left onto it. After nearly 200 yards, at a sharp left-hand bend, leave the track and take a waymarked path straight on, soon bearing left to reach a crossing track. Turn right onto this and follow it for some 300 yards, then, when a field comes into view to your right, turn left onto a crossing track. On leaving Great Wood, bear slightly right following a track to a corner of Ridge Wood where there is a superb view of the Hambleden Valley with Pheasant's Hill ahead and Colstrope half to your left. Now go straight on downhill for about 50 yards, then turn right into the wood and follow a well-worn path downhill. At the bottom edge of the wood, turn sharp right onto bridleway HA35, a terraced track, and follow it along the slope of the hill above Hambleden for about three-quarters of a mile, keeping left at a fork and climbing gradually. On crossing the top of the rise at the end of the ridge, turn left onto a crossing path by a yew tree, then, after about 70 yards, at a T-junction, turn right (still on HA35) and continue downhill. Near the bottom edge of the wood, ignore a crossing track and continue to a small gate. Do not go through this gate, but turn sharp left onto bridleway HA36 along the inside edge of the wood with fine views of the Thames between Henley and Mill End backed by Remenham Hill. Eventually you pass the rear of some cottages and reach a road. Turn right onto this and after about 100 yards turn left into a rough lane (path HA29a). Just before reaching a bridge over Hambleden Brook, turn left over a stile onto path HA30 and head for a cedar left of Hambleden Church to reach a kissing-gate by the road bridge over the brook at the entrance to the village. Turn right onto this road, passing the pump, the church and the 'Stag and Huntsman' to reach your starting point.

WALK 24: Hambleden (South)

Length of Walk: 6.9 miles / 11.1 Km
Starting Point: Entrance to public car park near 'Stag & Huntsman', Hambleden.
Grid Ref: SU785866
Maps: OS Landranger Sheet 175
OS Explorer Sheets 171 & 172 (or old Sheet 3)
OS Pathfinder Sheets 1156 (SU68/78) & 1157 (SU88/98)
Chiltern Society FP Maps Nos. 1 & 11
How to get there / Parking: See Walk 23.
Notes: In summer parts of the route may be overgrown with nettles.

Hambleden (see Walk 23) is not only a picturesque and historically interesting village in its own right, but also forms the gateway from the heart of the Buckinghamshire Chilterns to a particularly attractive section of the Thames Valley, a mile to the south.

This walk, indeed, takes you from the village over a wooded hillside where the Hambleden Valley meets the Thames Valley to the attractive riverside village of Medmenham, which is also rich in history. It then heads north into remote, heavily-wooded countryside leading you by way of Bockmer End to the site of the presumed lost hamlet of Holywick, before turning west across the plateau and dropping back down into Hambleden.

Starting from the entrance to the public car park in Hambleden, take path HA26 (part of the Chiltern Way) through the car park to some gates under chestnut trees at the far end of the car park. Here go through the handgate into a sports field and turn left, following a left-hand hedge at first, then continue uphill to a gap in the top hedge leading into a rough lane (path HA28). Turn right into this lane and follow it for a quarter mile. At a junction of lanes turn left, then after about 100 yards, fork right by a gate, keeping left of a hedge ahead and following it, later a field boundary, to a stile into Chainy House Plantation. Inside the wood, ignore a kissing-gate to the right and take path HA29 straight on along the edge of a plantation, then bear half left, following a waymarked path through a young plantation and

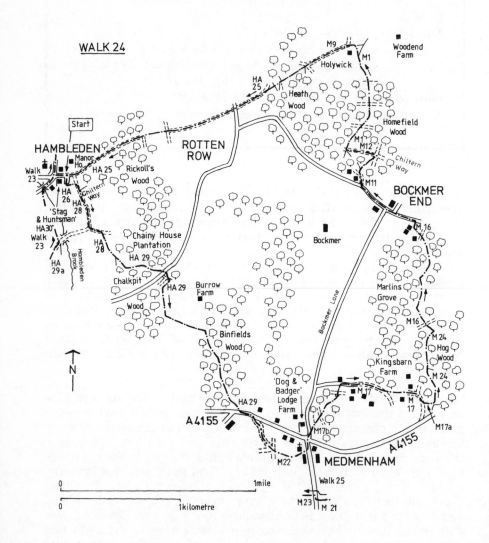

WALK 24

Start

HAMBLEDEN

ROTTEN ROW

BOCKMER END

Walk 23

Manor Ho.

HA 25

Rickoll's Wood

HA 26

HA 28

'Stag & Huntsman'

HA 30

Walk 23

HA 29a

HA 28

HA 29

Chainy House Plantation

Chalkpit

Wood

HA 29

Burrow Farm

Binfields Wood

HA 29

Hambleden Brook

Chiltern Way

Heath Wood

HA 25

M9

Holywick

M1

Woodend Farm

Homefield Wood

M1

M12

Chiltern Way

M11

M 16

Bockmer

Marlins Grove

M16

M 24

Hog Wood

M 24

Kingsbarn Farm

Bockmer Lane

'Dog & Badger' Lodge Farm

M 17

M 17

M17a

A 4155

M17b

M22

MEDMENHAM

A 4155

Walk 25

M 23

M 21

N

0 — 1 mile

0 — 1 kilometre

a strip of beechwood to reach a stile leading to a sunken lane. Cross this road bearing half right and follow path HA29 along the inside edge of Chalkpit Wood, disregarding two branching tracks to the right and reaching a corner of the wood. Here turn right and follow a left-hand fence along the edge of the wood. After some 300 yards, the path turns left between fences and crosses two fields, with the partly sixteenth-century Burrow Farm to the left, to join a grassy track leading into Binfields Wood. In the wood, follow a track bearing right and continuing for a quarter mile, eventually narrowing to a path and dropping steeply, ignoring a branching path to your right and continuing to a stile at the A4155 road. Cross this busy road carefully and turn left along its pavement. After 75 yards turn right through a hedge gap onto a waymarked permissive path, bearing left and following a grassy track around two sides of a field to a hedge gap and culvert. (N.B. If this permissive path is closed, continue along the A4155 to Medmenham crossroads). Now turn left over a stile by a gate and a footbridge onto path M22, crossing a private road and another stile and following a left-hand tree-belt to cross a further stile. Here follow a right-hand garden fence and wall straight on. Just before reaching a five-bar gate, bear slightly left, passing left of some sheds to reach a hedge gap into Ferry Lane, Medmenham.

Medmenham, most of which is situated along Ferry Lane and is thereby hidden from the main road, is a haven of rural peace. The church dates from the twelfth century, but has a fifteenth-century tower and chancel, while the 'Dog and Badger' is reputed to date from 1390 and the manor house was built by Geoffrey Pole in about 1450 and parts of the riverside abbey (see Walk 25) may be of thirteenth-century origin. There is, however, evidence of even earlier habitation as the hill you are about to climb is capped by an Iron Age hill fort which was later used as the site for the Norman Bolebec Castle.

Now turn left into Ferry Lane and at the crossroads by the church cross the A4155 again into Bockmer Lane and fork right off the road up the terraced path M17b. At the hilltop, having crossed the Iron Age fortification, continue straight on along an ill-defined path between pits until you reach a kissing-gate. Go through this, then turn left along a track. At a junction of tracks, go straight on through another kissing-gate, following a fenced path to School Lane opposite the front door of a house. Turn right along this road, passing the old village school with its bell and mullioned windows and ignoring all branching drives. Where the public road ends, take bridleway M17 (also a private road) straight on towards The Hermitage. On reaching its gateway, fork left onto a fenced bridleway and follow this downhill to a gate. Go through this and by Pheasantry Cottage, join its macadam drive, then, at a junction, turn right. Immediately on entering Hog Wood, turn left onto path M17a uphill through the wood to reach crossing terraced path M24. Turn left onto this, following it for nearly half a mile, after 350 yards ignoring a branching path to your right and eventually entering a plantation and dropping down to leave the wood by a stile. Cross this stile and turn right onto a farm track, then, by a gate ahead, turn left and take fenced path M16 uphill to a stile into a wood called Marlins Grove. Inside the wood, bear right and follow a waymarked path through it, eventually emerging at a stile. Cross this stile, a concrete farm road and another stile and bear half right across a field to cross a stile in the far right-hand corner of the field leading to a road at Bockmer End.

Turn left along this road and follow it for a third of a mile, disregarding branching roads to right and left and passing through the hamlet with its attractive old cottages. Just before Flint Cottage on the right, turn right into a lane to Woodside House (path M11). Go through a gate and where the lane bears left, leave it and take a path between hedges straight on into Homefield Wood. Inside the wood, fork half right and, ignoring a branching path to the right, follow the path downhill through a plantation. At the bottom of the hill, turn left into a wide fire break (path M12) joining the Chiltern Way. After about 250 yards, at the top of a slight rise, leaving the Chiltern Way, turn right onto waymarked path M1. Follow it uphill, ignoring two crossing tracks, to a stile at the edge of the wood. Cross this and follow a left-hand hedge through two fields, passing a pit, to reach some ruins at Holywick. Old documents refer to a thirteenth-century chapel having been here and this would suggest that Holywick may be the site of a lost hamlet.

Just past the ruins, turn left onto path M9, a grassy track and follow it beside a left-hand hedge into a valley. In the valley bottom, go straight on for 25 yards, then turn left over a stile into Heath Wood, immediately forking right and following the inside edge of the wood uphill. By the corner of the field to the right, keep left at a fork, crossing a stile and soon reaching a five-way junction. Here take a woodland path (still M9) straight on, ignoring a crossing path and eventually reaching a fence gap leading out of the wood. Now turn left onto a farm track (path HA25) and follow it for some 350 yards to a road. Having crossed this, take a macadam farm road straight on for over a third of a mile. Where the road turns right, leave it and take path HA25 straight on, following a grassy track beside a right-hand hedge to a gate and stile into Rickoll's Wood. Now ignore a branching track to the left and continue straight on downhill for nearly half a mile through the wood and along a rough lane, eventually reaching your starting point.

WALK 25: Mill End

Length of Walk: 9.8 miles / 15.8 Km

Starting Point: Entrance to public car park at Mill End.

Grid Ref: SU785854

Maps: OS Landranger Sheet 175
   OS Explorer Sheets 171 & 172 (or old Sheet 3)
   OS Pathfinder Sheets 1156 (SU68/78) & 1157 (SU88/98)
   Chiltern Society FP Maps Nos. 1 & 11 &
   East Berks RA FP Map No. 5

How to get there / Parking: Mill End, 4 miles west of
   Marlow, may be reached from the town by taking the
   winding A4155 towards Henley-on-Thames for 4.5 miles
   to Mill End, then turning right onto a road signposted to
   Hambleden, Skirmett and Fingest. A public car park is on
   the left just past the turning to Rotten Row.

Notes: This walk should not be attempted when the Thames
   is in flood, as parts of it are likely to be underwater.

Mill End, though today only a small riverside appendage of
Hambleden, is a settlement of considerable antiquity, as the
remains of a Roman villa were discovered here in 1911 and
during subsequent excavations of the site, evidence of earlier
Iron Age habitation was also found. Today the hamlet consists of
the early seventeenth-century Yewden Manor and a number of
attractive farms and cottages, but what the many visitors come
to see is the picturesque riverside scene with the lock, weir,
watermill and verdant islands, which is often considered to be
the most beautiful on the whole of the Thames. What many do
not realise, however, is that Mill End with its footbridge across
the Thames is also an ideal centre for walks along the valley and
over the surrounding hills and since the opening of the Temple
footbridge across the Thames in 1989 as part of preparations for
the Thames Path, walks using both sides of the river of under 10
miles are again possible in both directions which had not been
the case since the ancient ferries ceased to operate.

This walk, which is one of considerable beauty, takes you
first across the river to the Berkshire bank, by way of Aston,
Culham Court and the towpath to the fascinating historic
village of Hurley, before crossing Temple bridge back to the
Buckinghamshire side and returning via the equally historic
village of Medmenham to Mill End.

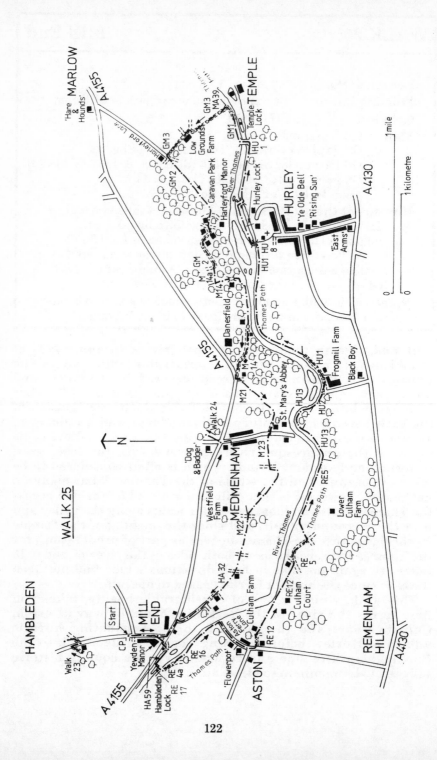

WALK 25

HAMBLEDEN

MARLOW

TEMPLE

HURLEY

MEDMENHAM

ASTON

REMENHAM HILL

MILL END

1 mile
1 kilometre

Starting from the entrance to the public car park at Mill End, cross the road and turn right along its footway. Where the footway transfers to the other side of the road by Yewden Manor, cross the road again and continue to the A4155. Turn right onto this road, then just past the entrance to Hambleden Marina, turn left onto path HA59, an alleyway between cottages leading to the marina drive. Follow the drive for a few yards, then bear slightly right into a fenced alleyway leading to the long footbridge over the weir and sluice gates with the white, early seventeenth-century weather-boarded watermill to your right. At the far end of this bridge, take path RE17 straight on across a small island to the lock, then continue over the lock gates to the Berkshire bank. Here turn left onto path RE4a, joining the Thames Path and passing through a kissing-gate, then follow a track along the riverbank. Where the track turns right away from the river, leave it and take path RE16 straight on through gates, following the riverbank until you reach a kissing-gate, footbridge and car park at the end of Ferry Lane opposite Hambleden Place. Now turn right into Ferry Lane and follow it for a quarter mile to the 'Flowerpot Hotel' in Aston.

Here take Aston Lane straight on and after about 80 yards, turn left onto path RE12, the macadam private road to Culham Court and Holme Farm. At a fork, keep right, then, by Holme Farm, where this road turns right, leave it and go straight on, soon passing through a kissing-gate where fine views open out of the Thames Valley to your left and Culham Court, a red-brick seventeenth-century Thames-side mansion ahead. Now follow the top of a slight bank straight on to a kissing-gate by Culham Court. Here bear slightly left and follow a right-hand fence past the house with its formal garden with balustrades and topiared hedges, passing through three further kissing-gates. Now go straight on across a field to pass the corner of a fence and a redundant handgate, then continue to a handgate onto a track (path RE5). Turn left onto this track, soon passing between bollards and joining a private road. Follow this, bearing right by a gate, then, at a junction of private roads, turn left through a kissing-gate and bear slightly right across a field to a kissing-gate and footbridge on the bank of the Thames. Cross these and then follow the riverbank for over 2 miles (on paths RE5, HU13, HU2 and HU1) to reach a footbridge over part of the Thames at Hurley.

On the way, you pass a number of interesting buildings including St. Mary's Abbey, Medmenham on the opposite bank. What you see today is, in fact, largely a Tudor house built by Francis Duffield in 1595, which was extensively restored in both 1745 and 1898, but some of its walls are believed to have formed part of the original thirteenth-century Cistercian abbey. In the mid-eighteenth century, this abbey achieved notoriety when it was rented by Sir Francis Dashwood, who later became Lord Le de Spencer, and was used for meetings of his Knights of St. Francis or Hellfire Club which were allegedly of an orgiastic nature. Be that as it may, he had the inscription 'Fay ce que voudras' quoted from the French poet, Rabelais, carved above the entrance, which does nothing to dispel the legend. Further on, you then pass the former Frognill Farm and Danesfield House on a cliff in trees which was built in the Italian renaissance style as recently as 1900.

On reaching the footbridge at Hurley, if wishing to visit the picturesque village, turn right down a flight of steps onto path HU8 and follow this macadam path into the village. To your left is the eleventh-century church and other buildings of the Norman priory where secret meetings in 1688 decided to invite William of Orange to come to England to displace James II. To your right is the ancient tithe barn and a fourteenth-century dovecote and further along the village street is the much-renovated 'Olde Bell' dating from 1135.

Otherwise, turn left over the footbridge (still on path HU1) to reach an island, then turn right and follow the bank of the island past Hurley Lock where you ignore a signposted branching path crossing the lock. At the far end of the island, cross a bridge back to the Berkshire bank, then turn left and follow the riverbank for over a third of a mile to cross the bridge over the Thames at the site of the former Temple Ferry. Now turn right onto path GM1 along the Buckinghamshire bank and follow it to Temple Lock. At the far end of the lock, take a track straight on along the riverbank with Bisham's twelfth-century church coming into view ahead. Where this track turns left and leaves the river, follow it (leaving the Thames Path and now on path MA39, later GM3) to Low Grounds Farm. Here follow the track turning right then left past a timber-framed barn, then take the macadam farm road straight on until you reach a cottage called East Lodge.

Turn left here onto path GM2 into Harleyford Park, soon crossing a stile by a large white gate. Now continue between fences to cross a macadam drive, then follow a right-hand fence straight on for nearly half a mile, at one point passing through a white wicket gate. On reaching a kissing-gate, where Harleyford Manor, a riverside mansion designed by Sir Robert Taylor in 1756 and visited in 1846 by Louis Napoleon, comes into view ahead, bear slightly right, following a right-hand wall, then keeping right of iron railings to reach a private road. Cross this and go through a gap left of the gates of Manor Joinery, then go straight on, keeping left of the buildings, ignoring a path between walls to your left and bearing slightly right up rough steps to reach a junction of macadam drives. Here take the macadam drive to the golf club straight on, bearing right by some cottages and passing through white gates onto a fenced gravel drive. Follow this, passing Home Farm House, then continuing through more white gates and along a fenced track along the edge of the golf course, eventually bearing right. Just before reaching a gate onto the golf course, turn left through a former kissing-gate onto path M14a into woodland and follow a left-hand fence downhill and up again. By large wooden gates, turn left and follow path M14 between a wall and a fence until you enter a tunnel. At the far end of the tunnel, go straight on along a fenced sunken path, soon emerging onto a terraced path which drops steeply to reach the River Thames near the Buckinghamshire end of Hurley Weir. On crossing a bridge over a small backwater, turn right, passing the Wittington Winch used to haul barges up a flash lock before the construction of Hurley Lock in 1774 and follow the fenced path straight on for a third of a mile until you reach a cottage at the bottom of the wooded cliff below Danesfield House. Here join a macadam drive and follow it for a third of a mile to reach the A4155. Turn left onto this road, then turn immediately left again onto path M21, the drive to Abbey Lodge. Having crossed a small bridge, by the lodge turn right through a gate, soon reaching a stile into the park of St. Mary's Abbey. Now bear half left across the parkland passing just right of three fenced young trees and crossing a stile left of some wooden sheds then keep straight on to a stile by a willow tree. Cross this and a second stile and take a fenced path to a gate and footbridge then continue between a fence and a stream passing a garage block to your left to reach a drive which you follow to Medmenham village street.

Turn right into the village street, crossing a bridge, then turn immediately left over a stile by a gate onto path M23, following a power-line through scrubland, eventually bearing right to cross a stile. Now follow a left-hand fence straight on to cross a stile by a gate and the drive to the Water Research Centre. Here continue between fences, then turn immediately left, soon turning left then right to reach a stile. Turn right over this stile and follow a right-hand hedge to a corner, then bear half right across a field passing left of a single oak tree to reach a crossing raised farm track by a gap in a belt of trees. Here join path M22 crossing the farm track and taking a track through the belt of trees, then continuing straight on across a field to a kissing-gate right of a low brick building. Now cross a concrete road and go straight on to a stile and fence gap right of the brick building. Here cross a concrete road, then go through a gap by a kissing-gate and bear slightly right onto path HA32 heading for the right-hand of two stiles in the far corner of the field. Cross this and follow a macadam drive, later a public road straight on to reach the A4155 at Mill End. Turn left onto this road and follow it to the Hambleden turn, then turn right for your starting point.

WALK 26:   Booker Common

Length of Walk: 8.3 miles / 13.4 Km
Starting Point: Booker Memorial Hall, Limmer Lane.
Grid Ref: SU835914
Maps: OS Landranger Sheet 175
            OS Explorer Sheet 172 (or old Sheet 3)
            OS Pathfinder Sheets 1138 (SU89/99) & 1157 (SU88/98)
            Chiltern Society FP Map No. 1
How to get there / Parking: Booker Common, 2 miles
    southwest of the centre of High Wycombe, may be reached
    by leaving the M40 at Junction 4 (Handy Cross) and
    taking the A4010 towards Aylesbury. At the third
    subsequent roundabout, turn left onto a road signposted to
    Lane End. After a mini-roundabout, take the next turning
    right (Limmer Lane). At a grass roundabout, turn left onto
    a rough road along the edge of Booker Common and find a
    suitable parking place.

Booker, on a hilltop southwest of the centre of High Wycombe,
is today known to most local people as a suburban sprawl of
housing estates, but many do not realise that hidden behind
these estates is an extensive, largely wooded rural common
surrounded by a scattering of typical old Chiltern cottages. In
fact, this common belonging to the West Wycombe Estate is of
considerable antiquity dating back at least 900 years and a
study of nineteenth- and early twentieth-century maps shows
it as the focal point of the scattered hamlet of Booker. It is
therefore only since the war that modern development has
swamped it and all but obliterated its former identity.

The walk, although initially traversing the modern
development, is little impaired by it, as, even before leaving
the town, fine views open out across the wooded country to
the south towards the Thames Valley and beyond and once
you have passed under the M40, an area of surprisingly remote
country to the west of the High Wycombe – Marlow road is
reached which this walk explores. After passing through
Marlow Bottom and skirting the edge of Marlow, the walk,
which is interspersed throughout with fine beechwoods, visits
the quiet hilltop hamlet of Copy Green and continues to
Bluey's Farm in its idyllic solitary bottom. You then return by

way of Widdenton Park Wood near Lane End to Booker's wooded common.

Starting from Booker Memorial Hall by the roundabout where Limmer Lane emerges onto Booker Common, take Limmer Lane southeastwards to reach the Lane End road, then turn left onto it. After about 100 yards, turn right onto path HW105, a narrow enclosed path. On reaching a road, cross it and take a gravel path straight on to reach a bend in a macadam path. Do not join this, but turn right onto a gravel path through a hedge gap, then turn immediately left and follow the edge of a playing field with fine views to your right across the M40 towards the Thames Valley around Maidenhead. At the far end of the playing field, bear slightly left up a bank and through a hedge gap, then continue along the top of a grassy bank past a car park, cross a road and take a fenced path straight on. On reaching a macadam path, turn right onto it, then ignore a branching path to the left and soon cross a road. Now take Holmers Lane straight on, passing the seventeenth-century former Holmer's Farm with its massive brick chimney typical of the period. At the end of the road, take bridleway HW140 straight on through a gate and down a hedged lane to the M40 fence. Here turn left along path HW144, a fenced track leading you to a tunnel under the motorway. At the far end of the tunnel, take path GM30 turning right along a fenced path, soon bearing left and later becoming a hedged lane which leads you downhill and up again to a junction of tracks at Oldhouse Farm.

Here take a macadamed road straight on, then at a junction, go straight on to reach a sharp right-hand bend near Ragman's Castle. Leave the road here and take bridleway GM39, a pleasant green lane, straight on with views to your right across the upper end of Marlow Bottom. Follow this lane straight on for a third of a mile passing Wymers Wood and reaching the macadam drive to Wymers. Cross this drive and go straight on for a further 200 yards to a fork. Here pause to look at a fine view of Marlow and the surrounding Thames Valley through a hedge gap, then turn right onto bridleway GM54 and follow this winding green lane for two-thirds of a mile gently descending until you reach a macadam road at the edge of Marlow Bottom, where pre-war ribbon development and more recent in-filling have combined to form a new village of some 5,000 inhabitants.

Follow this road straight on for about 70 yards, then, at a left-hand bend, turn right onto hedged bridleway GM50 joining the Chiltern Way. After about 120 yards, ignore a bollarded alleyway to your left, then, at a fork, keep right taking path GM50a, a fenced alleyway, straight on to New Road. Cross this road and take path GM50b, a further alleyway, straight on passing the end of a cul-de-sac to reach

Beechtree Avenue. Turn left onto this road and after some 30 yards, turn right onto path GM50c, following it through the remnants of a wood and steeply downhill to the road known as Marlow Bottom, where you turn left again. After about 120 yards, at a left-hand bend, turn right onto path GM49, another narrow alleyway, and follow it uphill to reach a crossing track. Here go straight on uphill along a fenced path, then the edge of a playing field to its top corner, then, briefly leaving the Chiltern Way, turn left onto a fenced path into a wood. After about 30 yards, turn right onto a fenced path (still GM49) and follow it to a road called Seymour Plain. Turn right onto this road, soon reaching the B482 and continuing along this round a left-hand bend. Now turn left into Seymour Court Lane, rejoining the Chiltern Way and passing the entrance to Seymour Court, built on the site of an earlier house reputed to have been the birthplace of Lady Jane Seymour, one of Henry VIII's wives and mother of Edward VI, and by High Rews Farm reaching a gateway on your left giving a fine view of Marlow.

Having left the Chiltern Way, where the road ends just beyond End Farm House, take bridleway GM52, a rough lane, straight on downhill, keeping right at a fork and later climbing again past Highruse Wood to reach the end of another road at Copy Farm. Turn right onto this road and follow it for nearly a quarter mile to Copy Green where the verges widen out with a cottage to your right. Here, at a right-hand bend, fork left onto bridleway GM23, a pleasant green lane winding downhill, keeping left at a fork to reach Mundaydean Bottom. At the bottom of the hill, fork right into Shillingridge Wood. Just inside the wood, turn right onto bridleway GM65 and follow this waymarked woodland track along the valley bottom at first, then gradually climbing the right-hand slope to reach a plantation, Here keep left at a fork and follow the edge of the plantation. Having passed a gate to your left, keep left at two further forks and take path GM22 straight on over a stile into a field where a fine view opens out of Bluey's Bottom. Now turn right to cross a series of two stiles in the corner of the field, then follow the right-hand hedge straight on along the top edge of the next field to a further stile at its far end. Cross this stile and take enclosed bridleway GM24 straight on past a row of cypresses, then bear half right to enter a wood. Just inside the wood, fork left onto bridleway GM29 leaving the wood through a bridlegate with fine views of the picturesque Bluey's Farm opening out to your left. The brick-and-timbered farmhouse dates from the seventeenth century, while the thatched farm cottages, though newer, enhance its setting.

Now continue straight on passing right of the thatched cottages and following the left-hand hedge along the valley bottom, later with

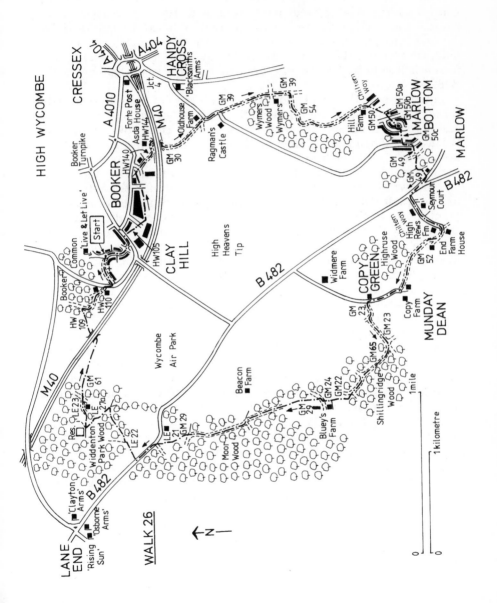

HIGH WYCOMBE

CRESSEX

HANDY CROSS

Blacksmiths' Arms'

Jct. 4

Forte Post
Asda House

Oldhouse Farm

Booker Turnpike

A 4010

M40

HW140

GM 30

HW144

Ragman's Castle

GM 39

Wymers' Wood

Wymers'

GM 39

Hill Farm

Chiltern Way

GM 50

GM 54

GM 50a
GM 50b
GM 50c

MARLOW BOTTOM

MARLOW

BOOKER

HW140

'Live & Let Live'

Start

Booker Common

HW105

CLAY HILL

HW C'

HW 109

HW 110

High Heavens Tip

GM 49

GM 49

Seymour Court

B 482

Widmere Farm

COPY GREEN

Highruse Wood

Chiltern Way

High Rews Fm

GM 52

End Farm House

B 482

Wycombe Air Park

GM 23

Copy Farm

GM 23

MUNDAY DEAN

M40

GM 61

LE 23

Res.

LE

Widdenton

Park Wood

GM 27a

LE 22

Beacon Farm

GM 65

Shillingridge Wood

GM 29

LE 21

Moor Wood

GM 24

GM 22

Bluey's Farm

GM 29

'Clayton Arms'

B 482

'Osborne Arms'

LANE END

'Rising Sun'

WALK 26

←N—

1 mile

1 kilometre

0

0

129

another hedge to your right, eventually entering Moor Wood. In the wood, follow a track straight on along the valley bottom for two-thirds of a mile ignoring one crossing path. On reaching a second where the main track turns left by a disused overgrown stile to your right, leave the track and follow the right-hand plantation fence straight on, later passing through mature woodland and reaching two bridlegates into a field. Go through these and take bridleway LE21 bearing slightly left to reach a gate and bridlegate by a corner of a wood leading to the B482.

Turn left onto this road and just over the brow of the hill, turn right through a hedge gap onto path LE22. Now go straight across a field and through a plantation, with views to your right towards Quarry Woods at Bisham and Maidenhead beyond, to reach a corner of the mature part of Widdenton Park Wood. Here turn right onto a defined path along the edge of mature beechwoods, later entering the woods and following their inside edge. After passing through the bottom of a dip, turn left onto path LE27a and follow it uphill along the edge of a plantation. At the far end of the plantation, bear slightly left into mature woodland following an ill-defined path until you reach a path junction near a corner of the wire-mesh fence surrounding an underground reservoir. Here turn right onto path LE23, immediately forking right again and ignoring a crossing track. On emerging into plantations, cross a stile and follow a right-hand fence to reach the drive to a shooting ground. Cross this and take a woodland path straight on beside a right-hand fence. On leaving the wood, cross a stile and take path GM61 straight on still beside the right-hand fence, then, where the fence turns right, leave it and go straight on across the field to reach a tunnel under the M40. Go through the tunnel and take path HW109 bearing half right across a field to a corner of woodland on Booker Common in a dip. Now follow an obvious path straight on through the wood until you reach a T-junction. Here turn right onto bridleway HW110 and follow it through the woods for nearly a quarter mile eventually emerging at a cottage. Now bear slightly right along a rough lane to reach Horns Lane. Turn right onto this road and follow it uphill for about 100 yards, then, before reaching the top, turn left onto the rough road along the edge of the common which leads you back to your starting point.

WALK 27:   Frieth

Length of Walk: 6.1 miles / 9.9 Km

Starting Point: 'Prince Albert', Moorend Common, Frieth.

Grid Ref: SU799906

Maps: OS Landranger Sheet 175
OS Explorer Sheet 171 (or old Sheet 3)
OS Pathfinder Sheets 1137 (SU69/79) & 1156 (SU68/78)
Chiltern Society FP Map No. 11

How to get there / Parking: Frieth, 4 miles northwest of Marlow, may be reached from the town by taking the B482 to Lane End and then turning left for Frieth. After 1 mile, at a crossroads in the bottom of a dip, turn right towards Fingest and look out for the 'Prince Albert' on your left after 300 yards. Cars can be parked along the edge of the common.

Frieth is, in some ways, an unusual village for the Chilterns as it is located on a hillside rather than on a ridgetop or in a valley bottom and its cottages are scattered around a network of narrow winding lanes with fields in between. This is probably explained by the fact that the village has always been a hamlet on the edge of Hambleden parish resulting from haphazard development rather than an independent parish and so instead of the cottages being built around the church, the church was only built in 1848 as a chapel-of-ease to serve the community which had grown up remote from the mother church in Hambleden.

The walk is one of great variety and exceptional beauty leading you through beechwoods before emerging at the top of a bank above Fingest with a spectacular view across the village and surrounding hills. After passing through the village, you then climb to Turville Hill where a further magnificent view of Turville and its valley awaits you, before descending to this picture-book village. The return route then takes you by way of Skirmett with further beechwoods alternating with fine views to reach the smaller-scale upland landscape around Frieth.

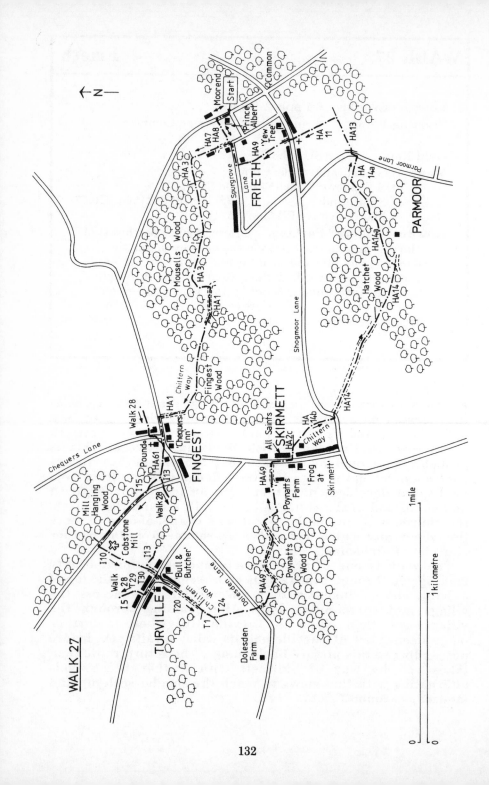

WALK 27

132

Starting from the 'Prince Albert' opposite Moorend Common at Frieth, take the road towards Fingest for about 100 yards. Opposite some cottages to the right, turn left over a stile onto path HA8 and follow a sporadic right-hand hedge uphill to a stile. Having crossed this stile, turn right into a lane (path HA7). Where the lane swings left, leave it and go straight on between hedges to enter Mousells Wood. Inside the wood, ignore a stile to your right and take path HA3 bearing left into the wood. Now continue straight on for nearly two-thirds of a mile disregarding all branching or crossing paths until you reach a rough lane. Turn right into the lane (path HA1) and follow it along the edge of the wood and then through it. Ignore branching paths to your left, joining the Chiltern Way and on reaching a gate and gap leading to a field, go through the gap and bear slightly right across the field to a waymarked path into Fingest Wood. Follow this path downhill through the wood to a gate and stile into a field by a seat where a superb view of the unspoilt village of Fingest and surrounding valleys opens out with the restored Cobstone Windmill on a hilltop ahead, the Stokenchurch Telecom Tower visible in the distance and Cadmore End on the ridge to your right.

Having stopped to admire this view, follow the outside edge of the wood downhill to a gate and stile. Cross this stile and continue along a grass track beside a left-hand hedge to gates and a stile leading onto a road on the edge of Fingest, then turn left into the village. The name Fingest is unusual as it derives from 'Thinghyrst', a name of Norse origin meaning 'meeting place in a spinney' and normally such names are only encountered in the areas conquered by the Vikings in the north and east of England. On entering the village, the seventeenth-century 'Chequers Inn' is on your left, but of particular interest is the largely unaltered twelfth-century church to your right with its unusually narrow lofty nave, its thick plastered walls and its tall Norman tower capped by a double saddleback roof, while along Chequers Lane to your right is the eighteenth-century village pound where stray animals were locked up to be redeemed on payment of a fine.

At the road junction, continue straight on past the church and 'Chequers Inn' (joining the route of Walk 28), then where the road begins to bear left, leave it and take path HA61 straight on over a stile. Now follow this enclosed path until you enter Mill Hanging Wood, then at a three-way fork, leaving the Chiltern Way, take the centre option, path I15 straight on uphill (leaving Walk 28 again) to reach a road. Turn right onto this and follow it up Turville Hill to reach Cobstone Mill on your left. Just past the windmill, turn left over a stile onto path I10, where Turville in its idyllic valley, now familiar to television viewers as 'Dibley', soon comes into view ahead and you follow a left-hand fence then a hedge dropping very steeply to a set of gates and stiles. Cross these stiles and follow a worn path straight on across a field to cross a further stile by a set of gates and rejoin the Chiltern Way. Now follow a rough track (path T30 briefly rejoining Walk 28) to reach the village street of Turville.

Although the name Turville has a French ring, it is, in fact, not of Norman origin, but a Norman corruption of the Anglo-Saxon name 'Thyrifield' (meaning 'Thyri's field') as the village is documented well before the Norman conquest. Indeed the church, whose fabric is in part eleventh-century, but has a sixteenth-century tower and has undergone other substantial alterations over the centuries, is believed to have replaced a Saxon predecessor as it has a Saxon font. It is also associated with a gruesome mystery, as, during renovation work in 1900, an old stone coffin was found hidden beneath the floor containing not only the skeleton of a thirteenth-century priest, but also the later remains of a woman with a bullet hole in her skull! Apart from the church, the village can also boast a fine selection of sixteenth- to eighteenth-century cottages, some of which are half-timbered and some brick-and-flint, and the picturesque timber-framed 'Bull and Butcher'.

Cross the village street passing left of a small green and, leaving Walk 28 again, take a narrow lane between the cottages. Where this macadam road ends, follow narrow bridleway T20 straight on between hedges to reach a large field. Now take bridleway T1 straight on beside a right-hand fence for about 150 yards to the top of a slight rise, then, leaving the Chiltern Way, bear half left onto path T24, heading for a stile just right of the near corner of a wood. Cross this stile, Dolesden Lane and a stile by a gate opposite and take path HA49 following a track to the entrance to a gas installation. Here bear slightly left soon leaving this wood, then go straight on uphill across a field to enter Poynatts Wood (named after the Poynant family who held Skirmett Manor in the fourteenth century). Now continue straight on uphill to reach a crossing track, then turn left onto it (still HA49) and follow it round the contours of the hill until you reach a junction with a sunken track. Bear half left onto this track and follow it downhill to a fence at the edge of the wood, then turn right and follow a fenced path along the edge of the wood with panoramic views to your left of Turville, Fingest, Skirmett and the surrounding hills. After about 130 yards the path turns left and leads you to a stile at Poynatts Farm. Cross this and go straight on along a lane to reach the village street at Skirmett with its attractive inns and cottages which like Fingest is unusual for its distinctly Norse name meaning 'shire meeting-place'.

Turn right along the village street passing the former Victorian church, now a house called 'All Saints', and just before the 'Frog at Skirmett', turn left onto path HA2, a lane by the village hall. Follow this lane to a bungalow, then cross a stile and briefly rejoining the Chiltern Way, bear half right onto path HA14b keeping left of a fence ahead. Where the fence bears away to the right, gradually diverge from it to reach a stile into Shogmoor Lane. Turn left onto this road, leaving the Chiltern Way again and at a bend, turn right onto sunken bridleway HA14 and follow it climbing gradually with views to your right of the Hambleden Valley. After nearly half a mile, on entering Hatchet Wood, fork right onto a sunken path. When you reach the far side of the wood, turn left onto path HA14a, a waymarked woodland path and follow it for nearly half a mile ignoring all lesser branching paths, until you cross a stile leading out of the wood. Here follow a left-hand fence straight on to a stile leading to Parmoor Lane. Turn left onto this road and after about 50 yards, turn right over a stile onto path HA13. Here ignore a second stile to your left and follow the left-hand hedge straight on for some 250 yards to a stile in the hedge at a junction of hedges. Turn left here over two stiles onto path HA11 and follow a fenced path straight on past Frieth Church to reach the village street where a topiared yew tree to your right marks the 'Yew Tree' pub. Cross this road and take path HA9, a grassy drive straight on to a stile, then follow a left-hand hedge straight on. At the far end of the field, cross a stile leading to a fenced path and follow this through two fields to a stile into Spurgrove Lane. Turn right onto this road, then at a sharp bend, go straight on over a stile onto path HA8 and retrace your outward route downhill to a road where you turn right for the 'Prince Albert'.

WALK 28:   Cadmore End

Length of Walk: 5.5 miles / 8.9 Km
Starting Point: Cadmore End Church.
Grid Ref: SU784926
Maps: OS Landranger Sheet 175
OS Explorer Sheet 171 (or old Sheet 3)
OS Pathfinder Sheet 1137 (SU69/79)
Chiltern Society FP Map No. 11
How to get there / Parking: Cadmore End, 5 miles west
of High Wycombe, may be reached by leaving the M40 at
Junction 5 (Stokenchurch), taking the A40 into
Stokenchurch, forking right onto the B482 towards
Marlow and following it for 2.5 miles. One-third of a mile
beyond the 'Blue Flag', by Cadmore End School, turn right
into a cul-de-sac to Cadmore End Church. Cars can be
parked at various points along this road.

Cadmore End, like many Chiltern 'ends', is built around an
ancient upland common straddling the ancient county
boundary between Oxfordshire and Buckinghamshire. Like
many such settlements, Cadmore End is distinctly
higgledy-piggledy with stretches of common separating its
scattered clusters of attractive Chiltern cottages. Its church
was built in 1851 in traditional local flint to replace a
mediaeval chapel on the site of the lost village of
Ackhampstead, two miles southeast of Cadmore End, which
had closed in 1849. Both villages had previously been detached
manors of distant Lewknor and with the building of this new
church, Cadmore End became an independent ecclesiastical
parish.

The walk, which is one of high scenic quality and superb
views, leads you down from the Cadmore End plateau to the
picture-book villages of Fingest and Turville, before returning
by way of the outskirts of Ibstone and its lofty ridge to
Cadmore End.

Starting from the end of the macadam road by Cadmore End Church, follow its stony continuation for a quarter mile, bearing left and passing clusters of cottages, until you emerge onto the B482 opposite the 'Old Ship'. Cross this road and turn right along its pavement. At a bend at the top of the hill by a lane to the left and a double cottage, recross the B482 and take path LE9, the track to Rackley's Farm. By a cattle grid, cross a stile and bear half right across a small field to pass right of a pond in the far corner. Here cross a stile into a path between a hedge and a fence and follow this to another stile into a field. Continue straight on beside a hedge until a stile takes you into a copse on the right. Now follow a winding path through the copse leading you to another stile. Cross this and turn right across the corner of a field to a double stile. Having crossed this, go straight on across the next field making for the corner of a hedge just left of a flint cottage beyond it. On reaching this corner, bear half right onto path LE8, following the hedge to a stile in a corner of the field. Cross this and follow a track straight on beside the left-hand hedge through a series of three gates, then crossing a stile by a fourth into a lane. Go straight on along the lane (path HA66), ignoring a left-hand branch to Hanger Farm. On joining bridleway HA65 coming out of Hanger Wood to your right, follow it straight on to a stile ahead at a sharp left-hand bend. From this stile the picturesque village of Fingest comes into view ahead clustered in a hollow where four valleys meet. (For a description, see Walk 27). Cross this stile and take path HA64 straight on beside a left-hand fence through a field then cross a stile and take a fenced path straight on to enter an alleyway (path HA63) leading to a village street in Fingest.

Turn left onto this road, then turn right through a kissing-gate onto path HA62 crossing the churchyard diagonally to another kissing-gate leading to a road where you join Walk 27 and the Chiltern Way. A few yards along the road, fork right over a stile onto path HA61 between a wall and a fence. Follow this, climbing gently, into Mill Hanging Wood. On entering the wood, fork left onto path 113 (leaving Walk 27), soon crossing a road flanked by stiles and take a confined path for a quarter mile with Turville Hill to the right and a narrow belt of trees to the left permitting glimpses of the Hambleden Valley. At the end of this section, cross a stile where Turville, now familiar to television viewers as 'Dibley', comes into view in the valley ahead. Bear half left across the field heading for the near corner of a fenced garden then bear slightly right and follow the garden fence to a field corner. Here turn left over a stile and take path T30 down a rough lane, briefly rejoining Walk 27, to reach Turville village green. (For a description of Turville, see Walk 27.)

Turn right along the village street (leaving Walk 27 and the

Chiltern Way) and follow it for about 150 yards. Opposite a black barn with a small turret on the roof and an enamel sign 'Air Raid Wardens' Post', turn right between cottages onto path T29, the path to Barn Cottage. Passing the cottage, climb steps and cross a stile, then take path I5, bearing half left across a field to a stile in the far corner. Having climbed this and another stile, cross the corner of a field and a stile into a belt of trees. Once among the trees, keep left at a fork, following a waymarked path soon swinging right and climbing a scrubby hillside diagonally to a further stile. Cross this and bear half right to a stile in the fence along the edge of a wood in an indentation hidden by a rise in the ground. Having crossed this, turn left and follow a fenced path along the edge of the wood, ignoring a branching path into the wood. Where the fence ends, turn right onto a track into the wood, then turn immediately left with a plantation to your left. Just past the far end of this plantation, turn right onto a waymarked path (still I5) and follow it through a new plantation. After about a quarter mile, the path bears right through an older plantation to reach a road on the edge of Ibstone.

Turn right onto this road, passing eighteenth-century Ibstone House, former home of the authoress, Dame Rebecca West. At the end of its garden, turn left through wooden gates onto bridleway I11, following a track beside a left-hand hedge soon crossing a drive. Here the track becomes fenced on both sides and descends through a copse to a gate. Go through this and follow a grassy track lined with fence posts straight on downhill passing a ruined barn, then bearing right then left down a parkland field to a gate and bridlegate into a belt of trees. Once among the trees, turn right onto bridleway I14c and follow it, ignoring a branching track to the left. After nearly 200 yards, at a fork keep left and follow the left-hand edge of the wood straight on until you emerge onto the edge of the wood. Now take fenced bridleway LE60 along the edge of the wood, then continue between fences, later with a hedge to your right. On passing through a hedge gap continue along fenced bridleway I14b on the other side of the hedge to a bridlegate then continue through a strip of woodland to reach Chequers Lane at Gravesend. Turn right onto this road, then, at a right-hand bend, turn left over a stile and take path LE2 across a field climbing to a stile into Hanger Wood. Inside the wood, follow the waymarked path keeping left at a fork then continuing uphill. At the top of the hill, ignore a branching track to your left and bear slightly right, then, at a T-junction, turn left onto path LE5 and follow it straight on to a gate at the edge of the wood. Go through this and bear slightly left onto bridleway LE7, then follow this winding track uphill back to Cadmore End.

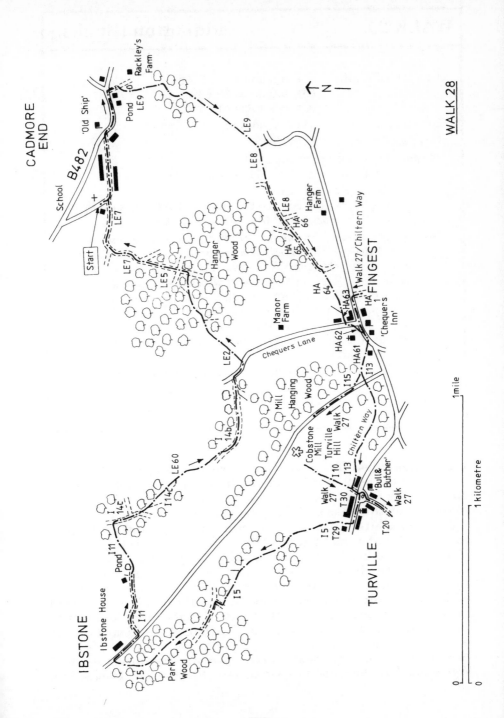

WALK 29:   Piddington (Bucks.)

Length of Walk: (A) 8.6 miles / 13.8 Km
                      (B) 5.0 miles / 8.1 Km
                      (C) 6.5 miles / 10.5 Km

Starting Point: 'Dashwood Arms', Piddington.

Grid Ref: SU807943

Maps: OS Landranger Sheets 165 & 175
OS Explorer Sheets 171 (all) & 172 (A/C only)
(or old Sheet 3 (all))
OS Pathfinder Sheets 1137 (SU69/79) & 1138 (SU89/99)
Chiltern Society FP Maps Nos. 7 & (A/B only) 11

How to get there / Parking: Piddington, some 3.5 miles west of the centre of High Wycombe, may be reached from the town by taking the A40 towards Oxford and turning left for the village on a loop road which marks the former course of the A40, before the village was bypassed. Cars can be parked at various points along this loop road, but the car park behind the 'Dashwood Arms' should not be used, as it is a private car park for customers and users of the recreation ground.

Notes: Heavy nettle growth may be encountered in the summer months particularly on path S53 in Fillington Wood on Walks A & B.

Piddington, just off the A40 Oxford road, is an unusual village for the Chilterns as it is largely built of red brick and is located on a hillside rather than in a valley bottom or on a ridgetop or plateau. For this reason, its appearance more closely resembles a West Yorkshire village than a Chiltern village and in the past the presence of a tall factory chimney added to this impression. Herein indeed lies the key to the village's appearance as, unlike other Chiltern villages, it only originated in 1903 as a settlement to house workers at the now-closed North's furniture factory which was built at the same time. It was therefore constructed in the style of industrial settlements of that period and not in that characteristic of older Chiltern villages. Its location here away from previously existing settlements can also be explained by the fact that North's previous premises in West Wycombe had become too small and Sir George Dashwood, who owned the village, objected to the erection of a larger factory there with such a chimney.

Despite the somewhat unpromising nature of Piddington itself, all three walks soon lead you into the quiet Chiltern backland to the west and north of the village with its steep-sided ridges offering some superb views across the hilltops, narrow 'bottoms' and a wealth of pleasant woodland.

Starting from the 'Dashwood Arms' at the western end of the Piddington loop road, **Walks A & B** turn left into the Wheeler End road. After a few yards, turn right onto bridleway PW1 and follow this winding rough track beside a left-hand hedge, later a fence to Fillington Farm, where it twists to the right, but does not enter the farm. Now ignore two branching tracks to your left and go straight on past a woodyard, then bear slightly left, soon joining a left-hand hedge. Where the hedge then turns right, turn left through the second of two adjacent field entrances onto path S52, following a left-hand hedge to a gap into a belt of trees called Tipping Shaw. Here fork immediately left onto path PW4 through the trees, then follow a left-hedge uphill. After a short distance, the hedge and path (now S94) gradually enter a combe, passing a thick hedge climbing the hill to the left. About 60 yards beyond this, turn left over an inconspicuous stile in the hedge onto path PW3 bearing half right up a bank to a gate and stile in the top right-hand corner of the field. Cross the stile and follow an old grassy track over the top of the hill, passing left of a hawthorn bush and a twin-poled wooden pylon. At the hilltop, before continuing, it is worth standing still and surveying the panoramic views. Where the track forks, bear half left towards Laurel Farm to cross a stile by a gate. Head for the right-hand end of the farm buildings, then keep right of the farm, crossing two stiles by the buildings and emerging onto a road at Wheeler End by its extensive common.

Turn right onto the road and follow it for a quarter mile past the 'Brickmakers Inn' and into a dip. After passing through the dip, just beyond the first left-hand cottage, turn right onto path LE42 across Cadmore End Common, swinging left and ignoring three branching paths to the right. At a crossways, go straight on down a slope into a small copse. Now bear slightly left, ignoring a parallel path to the right, then continue straight on, disregarding all branching or crossing paths until, just past a wooden bungalow to your right, you reach a fork. Here keep right, soon reaching a stony track. Turn right onto this, joining path LE34 and bearing left then right past a row of cottages to reach a macadam road. Turn left onto this and where it turns right, follow it, now on path LE36. After 100 yards, by a telegraph pole, turn left over a stile and follow a left-hand fence to the corner of a wood, then continue to a stile into it. Cross this stile and follow a path to cross two further stiles flanking a track, then continue through a finger of woodland until you leave it by a further stile. Here turn right onto path LE57, a rough track, and follow it for nearly half a mile along the ridge (soon becoming S53), with fine views ahead and to your left, to reach a corner of Barn Wood. Now turn left along its outside edge and after 10 yards, fork right onto path S53a into the wood. Follow this obvious waymarked path straight on downhill through the wood, ignoring a path merging from the left (where you rejoin S53) and continuing to a crossways in the valley bottom. Here disregard a crossing path and bear slightly left to cross a stile into the corner of a field, then follow the outside edge of the wood, later a hedge uphill to the top of the rise. Where the hedge bears slightly left, go slightly right heading for a stile into Fillington Wood ahead to cross a bridleway in the valley bottom. Here go straight on uphill to the stile into the wood, then follow a winding path through the wood for some 350 yards, eventually passing a redundant stile. Now ignore a branching path to the right and go straight on for a further 300 yards to a waymarked T-junction where you bear slightly right onto bridleway S89 to reach the A40 at Studley Green.

Cross this fast road carefully and turn right along its pavement. After some 40 yards, turn left through a kissing-gate onto path S72a and follow a left-hand hedge for over a third of a mile, crossing a series of stiles until you drop down to cross a stile into Bottom Wood, which, thanks to the generosity of Mrs Cynthia Ercolani, is now owned and cared for by the Chiltern Society. Here follow path RA29 beside a left-hand fence to a gate in the valley bottom where you turn right onto bridleway RA30. For **Walk A**, after 100 yards, by the corner of the left-hand field, turn left onto path RA32a and omit the next two paragraphs.

Walk B now follows bridleway RA30, later RA31, along the valley bottom through Bottom Wood for two-thirds of a mile. Having passed bridleway S90 to your right, by an old gatepost, you enter a wood called Plomer's Bottom and take bridleway PW27 straight on along the valley bottom for a further half mile, going through one gate and eventually another into a field. Now go straight on across the field to a gate and bridlegate leading to a track. Turn left onto this track following a left-hand hedge. Where the track forks by a barn at Ham Farm, go right, along a fenced track to a gate and bridlegate, then keep straight on to reach the A40 opposite the 'Dashwood Arms'.

Walk C also starts from the 'Dashwood Arms' and crosses the A40. Now take bridleway PW27, the centre option of three tracks, passing through a gate and bridlegate just left of the buildings at Ham Farm. Here go straight on through a second gate and bridlegate and take a fenced track, soon merging with a track from your right. On emerging into a field, follow the track beside a right-hand hedge to a gate and a bridlegate at the start of a row of oaks. Here turn right through the bridlegate and bear half left, following a defined track across the field to a gate into a wood called Plomer's Bottom. In the wood, at a fork, follow the left-hand track straight on along the valley bottom for half a mile, passing through another gate and later reaching a junction of bridleways by the corner of a left-hand field. Now take bridleway RA31, later RA30, straight on along the valley bottom through Bottom Wood for over half a mile ignoring all branching paths. On reaching a Chiltern Society noticeboard to your left, ignore a branching path to the right, then, by the corner of a right-hand field, turn right onto path RA32a to join **Walk A.**

Walks A and C now take path RA32a uphill along the inside edge of the wood to a stile. Cross this and follow a left-hand hedge straight on uphill to a stile where you join a fenced track and continue straight on to Ashridge Farm. Here take the track straight on between the buildings to a junction near a pond, then go straight on through a gate into a field and bear half right to a kissing-gate in the far corner onto Green End Road, Radnage. Turn left onto this road and after 100 yards, opposite the second pair of semi-detached houses on the left, turn right onto path RA26 between a hedge and a fence, continuing between hedges to emerge into a field. Here follow a right-hand hedge, later a fence, straight on downhill with fine views towards Bledlow Ridge ahead and later towards West Wycombe Church with its golden ball on a hilltop to your right. On passing the end of a copse, continue to follow the right-hand hedge downhill and up again to a hedge gap leading to a terraced road. Turn left along this road, then, just beyond the far end of the left-hand field, turn right onto path B69 climbing steeply through woodland to a stile. Now take a fenced path straight on uphill to cross a stile into Bledlow Ridge village cricket field, where you follow the left-hand hedge straight on, later passing tennis courts and a children's playground to reach the ridgetop road at Bledlow Ridge.

Cross this road and turn right along its pavement, soon passing a pond. Where the pavement ends, continue along the verge until you reach a road called Scrubbs Lane. Turn left into this and follow it downhill. At its end, go straight on over a stile by a gate onto path B71 and follow a right-hand hedge downhill through two fields and along a fenced track to reach Slough Lane. Turn left onto this road and follow it round a right-hand bend to Bottom Farm with its weatherboarded barns. Just past the farm, turn right over a stile by a gate onto path B86 and bear half left uphill, heading just left of the far corner of the field, to reach a terraced path into the trees to a stile into Allnutt's

Wood. Now take the waymarked path straight on through the wood to reach a crossing macadam drive (path B85). Turn right onto this and follow it for nearly half a mile, soon with a field to your right, to reach the end of the drive at Noble's Farm. Now take a track straight on through Hearnton Wood, which is believed to conceal the site of the lost village of Averingdown of which its name might be a corruption, for nearly another half mile with a fine view of Bradenham's Norman church and much-altered sixteenth-century manor house to your left at one point, until you reach a waymarked crossways.

Here turn right onto path B89, a grassy track leading you over the top of the ridge into a plantation. On reaching a crossing track, take a narrower path straight on into the trees which soon starts to drop to reach a handgate into a downland field. Go through this and bear half left onto an eroded path descending steeply through this nature reserve into an area of scrubland. Now go through a handgate and follow a hedged path to Slough Lane. Cross this road and a stile opposite, then follow a crop-break across a field with a closer view of West Wycombe Church on a hill to your left, to a gate and stile onto the Bledlow Ridge road. Having crossed this road and a further stile, follow a right-hand fence towards the early seventeenth-century, timber-framed Chorley Farm. Where the fence turns right, bear half right to a gate and stile opposite the farm.

Cross the stile and bear half left across the road to enter a flinty lane (bridleway WW11). Now follow this lane (soon becoming PW17) uphill into Chawley Wood. At the far side of the wood, where the lane bears left, leave it, taking path PW24 straight on through a hedge gap, then bearing left and following the left-hand hedge. Just before a corner of the field, go through a gap in the hedge and follow its other side to a handgate. Go through this, then turn left and follow a left-hand fence, ignoring a crossing track and eventually crossing a stile. Now go straight on through a hedge gap and follow a left-hand hedge downhill. At the bottom end of the field, cross some hurdles and a stile, then follow a right-hand fence straight on downhill to reach a gate and stile at the back of Ham Farm. Cross this stile into the farmyard, then, at its far side, turn left through a gate and bridlegate onto bridleway PW27 for the A40 and the 'Dashwood Arms'.

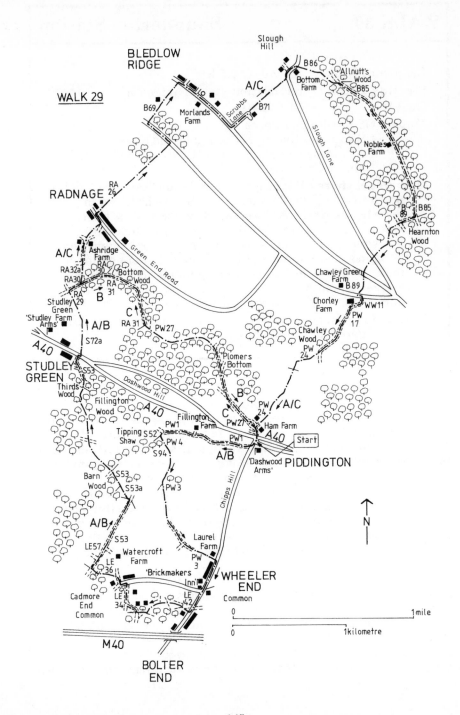

WALK 30:   Saunderton Station

Length of Walk: 5.3 miles / 8.5 Km
Starting Point: Saunderton Station approach.
Grid Ref: SU813981
Maps: OS Landranger Sheet 165
      OS Explorer Sheets 171 & 172 (or old Sheet 3)
      OS Pathfinder Sheets 1137 (SU69/79) & 1138 (SU89/99)
      Chiltern Society FP Map No. 7

How to get there / Parking: Saunderton Station, 4.5 miles
north-west of High Wycombe, may be reached from the
town by taking the A40 westwards for two miles, then
forking right onto the A4010 towards Aylesbury and
following it for 2.5 miles. Turn left onto a road signposted
to Saunderton Bottom and Deanfield and after passing
under a railway bridge, turn immediately right into the
station approach. If there are no parking spaces free here,
park in the neighbouring residential road.

Notes: In the summer months, heavy nettle growth may be
encountered in several places.

Saunderton Station would seem to be curiously situated, being
nearly three miles from the principal settlements of this
scattered parish which are, in fact, considerably closer to
Princes Risborough Station! Rather than the station being
built to serve Saunderton village, a new settlement with
several factories has grown up around the station.

The walk, which, in contrast to many in the Chilterns, is very
open in nature, takes you along the wide Saunderton valley to
Saunderton Lee near Lodge Hill, before climbing over Bledlow
Ridge to Radnage Church in its secluded valley. It returns over
another part of Bledlow Ridge to Slough Hill and Saunderton
Station.

Starting from the approach road to Saunderton Station, go down the
approach and turn right into Slough Lane. On reaching a left-hand
hairpin bend near some cottages, turn right into a field entrance, then
bear immediately left through a hedge gap. On entering a field, take
path B48, bearing half right and following a right-hand hedge towards
a corner of the field. Just before reaching it, turn right through a gap

in the hedge and cross the corner of the next field, rejoining the hedge at the top of a rise. Follow the hedge straight on for a few yards. Where it turns right, go straight on across the field, rejoining the hedge by the corner of Molins' factory fence. Here continue along a wide track between the hedge and the fence to Haw Lane. Cross this and take path B48 straight on through a hedge gap and across a field, walking parallel to the railway to your right until, level with the far side of Grange Farm on the other side of the railway, you bear slightly left across the field, heading towards two distant electricity pylons, to a hedge gap with a redundant stile step under a crabtree. Go through this and follow a right-hand hedge to Manor Farm, Saunderton Lee. Here bear half right onto a track through the hedge, ignoring a right-hand turn into the farmyard, and continue straight on past a thatched cottage and over a stile.

Just past the far end of a right-hand barn, by a telegraph pole, turn left onto path B47, passing left of a tree, then following a left-hand hedge until you reach a stile at the base of a pylon. Cross the stile and go straight on, following a right-hand hedge to a crossing track by a hedge. Lodge Hill, to the right, has a rather unusual appearance, rising up on its own out of the Saunderton valley and not being part of a Chiltern ridge. It is of interest for a number of ancient earthworks and the discovery there of Neolithic tools, Bronze Age pottery and other relics.

Continue straight on over a stile and across a field to the next hedge, where you turn left onto a grassy track (bridleway B55). Follow this past Lodge Hill Farm to the right joining a macadam drive, then turn right onto path B61, a macadam farm road leading to a barn at the far end of the farm. By the barn, fork left along a concrete road, then, just before a farm gate, turn left through a kissing-gate and follow a right-hand hedge to a gate and stile. Cross the stile and heading slightly right of diagonally, go uphill across a field, making for a gate and stile under some trees left of a house, when these come into view. Here cross the stile and go straight on up a lane to the spine road of Bledlow Ridge.

Turn right onto the road and, where the houses to the left end, turn left over a stile onto path B60, following the left-hand hedge downhill. In the corner of the field, cross a stile into a thicket and turn right through this thicket, soon emerging in a scrubby downland field. Follow the right-hand hedge downhill to a stile in bushes in the bottom corner. Cross this stile and continue straight on across the next field to a stile leading to Radnage Lane. Turn left onto this road and after 300 yards turn left again up the drive to Radnage Church.

Take path RA6 straight on through a gate into the churchyard. The thirteenth-century church has a Saxon font dug up in a field nearby and is notable for a thirteenth-century mural, discovered beneath later murals during restoration work.

Bear right of the church to a stile in the stone wall at the back corner of the churchyard. Having crossed this, bear half right across a field to another stile. Bear slightly left across a further field to cross another stile, then take path B66a, bearing half left across the next field to a stile at the point where the bottom edge of Yoesden Wood appears to drop down. Cross this and follow a right-hand fence uphill, turning right where it does. Now follow a worn path, soon bearing left and climbing steeply along the left-hand edge of a scrubby downland field through bushes with magnificent views behind towards Stokenchurch, Andridge and the back of the escarpment, and enter the wood at the top corner of the field. Go straight on through the wood, ignoring a stile at one point. On reaching the corner of a field, turn left onto path B66 between a hedge and a fence and follow this to a road at Bledlow Ridge.

Here cross the road and turn right along its pavement. After 100 yards, just past the entrance to a house called Waverley, turn left onto path B64 between a fence and a hedge. On emerging into fields, continue between fences to a stile, then follow a left-hand hedge downhill. Where the hedge turns left, bear half right across the field to a stile in the corner. Having crossed this, follow a right-hand hedge downhill to cross a stile. Now bear slightly right across a field to the right-hand end of a garden hedge to reach a gate onto a farm road (bridleway B55). Turn right onto this and follow it to Haw Lane, onto which you turn left. At the top of a rise, turn right over a stile onto path B49 and follow a right-hand hedge uphill through three fields. At the top of Slough Hill by a spreading beech tree, cross a stile and bear half left onto path B50 through a hedge gap, then go straight on across a field towards the Janssen-Clag building with its flagpoles to a hedge gap in front of a cottage leading to Slough Lane, along which you retrace your steps to Saunderton Station.

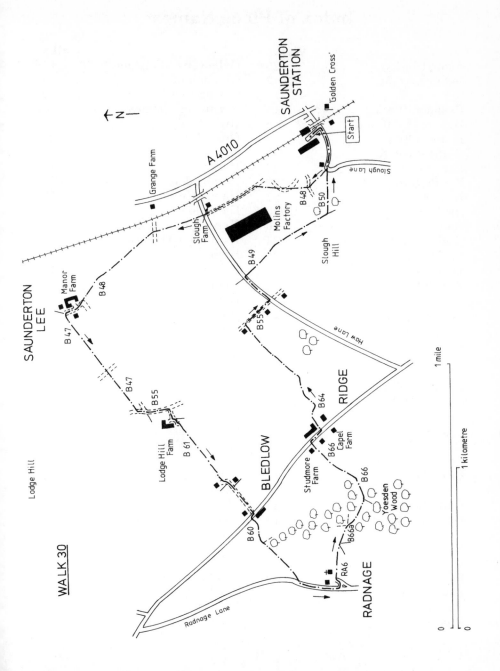

WALK 30

SAUNDERTON
LEE

SAUNDERTON
STATION

Golden Cross

Start

Slough Lane

A 4010

Grange Farm

Slough
Farm

Molins
Factory

Slough Hill

B 48

B 50

B 49

Manor
Farm

B 48

B 47

B 47

B 55

B 55

How Lane

Lodge Hill

Lodge Hill
Farm

B 61

B 64

RIDGE

BLEDLOW

B 60

Studmore
Farm

B 66
Capel
Farm

B 66

Yoesden
Wood

B 66a

RA6

RADNAGE

Radnage Lane

N

0   1 kilometre

0   1 mile

149

Index of Place Names

Books Published by THE BOOK CASTLE

CHANGES IN OUR LANDSCAPE: Aspects of Bedfordshire, Buckinghamshire and the Chilterns 1947-1992: Eric Meadows. Over 350 photographs from the author's collection spanning nearly 50 years.

COUNTRYSIDE CYCLING IN BEDFORDSHIRE, BUCKINGHAMSHIRE AND HERTFORDSHIRE: Mick Payne. Twenty rides on and off-road for all the family.

PUB WALKS FROM COUNTRY STATIONS: Bedfordshire and Hertfordshire: Clive Higgs. Fourteen circular country rambles, each starting and finishing at a railway station and incorporating a pub stop at a mid way point.

PUB WALKS FROM COUNTRY STATIONS: Buckinghamshire and Oxfordshire: Clive Higgs. Circular rambles incorporating pub-stops.

LOCAL WALKS: South Bedfordshire and North Chilterns: Vaughan Basham. Twenty-seven thematic circular walks.

LOCAL WALKS: North and Mid Bedfordshire: Vaughan Basham. Twenty-five thematic circular walks.

FAMILY WALKS: Chilterns South: Nick Moon. Thirty 3 to 5 mile circular walks.

FAMILY WALKS: Chilterns North: Nick Moon. Thirty shorter circular walks.

CHILTERN WALKS: Hertfordshire, Bedfordshire and North Bucks: Nick Moon.

CHILTERN WALKS: Buckinghamshire: Nick Moon.

CHILTERN WALKS: Oxfordshire and West Buckinghamshire: Nick Moon. A trilogy of circular walks, in association with the Chiltern Society. Each volume contains 30 circular walks.

OXFORDSHIRE WALKS: Oxford, the Cotswolds and the Cherwell Valley: Nick Moon.

OXFORDSHIRE WALKS: Oxford, the Downs and the Thames Valley: Nick Moon. Two volumes that complement Chiltern Walks: Oxfordshire, and complete coverage of the county, in association with the Oxford Fieldpaths Society. Thirty circular walks in each.

THE D'ARCY DALTON WAY: Nick Moon. Long-distance footpath across the Oxfordshire Cotswolds and Thames Valley, with various circular walk suggestions.

THE CHILTERN WAY: Nick Moon. A guide to the new 133 mile circular Long-Distance Path through Bedfordshire, Buckinghamshire,Hertfordshire and Oxfordshire, as planned by the Chiltern Society.

JOURNEYS INTO BEDFORDSHIRE: Anthony Mackay. Foreword by The Marquess of Tavistock, Woburn Abbey. A lavish book of over 150 evocative ink drawings.

COCKNEY KID & COUNTRYMEN: Ted Enever. The Second World War remembered by the children of Woburn Sands and Aspley Guise. A six year old boy is evacuated from London's East End to start life in a Buckinghamshire village.

BUCKINGHAM AT WAR: Pip Brimson. Stories of courage, humour and pathos as Buckingham people adapt to war.

WINGS OVER WING: The Story of World War II Bomber Training Unit: Mike Warth. The activities of RAF Wing in Buckinghamshire.

JOURNEYS INTO BUCKINGHAMSHIRE: Anthony Mackay. Superb line drawings plus background text: large format landscape gift book.

BUCKINGHAMSHIRE MURDERS: Len Woodley. Nearly two centuries of nasty crimes.

WINGRAVE: A Rothschild Village in the Vale: Margaret and Ken Morley. Thoroughly researched and copiously illustrated survey of the last 200 years in this lovely village between Aylesbury and Leighton Buzzard.

HISTORIC FIGURES IN THE BUCKINGHAMSHIRE LANDSCAPE: John Houghton. Major personalities and events that have shaped the county's past, including Bletchley Park.

TWICE UPON A TIME: John Houghton. North Bucks short stories loosely based on fact.

SANCTITY AND SCANDAL IN BEDS AND BUCKS: John Houghton. A miscellany of unholy people and events.

MANORS and MAYHEM, PAUPERS and PARSONS: Tales from Four Shires: Beds., Bucks., Herts. and Northants: John Houghton. Little known historical snippets and stories.

THE LAST PATROL: Policemen killed on duty while serving the counties of Berkshire, Buckinghamshire and Oxfordshire: Len Woodley.

FOLK: Characters and Events in the History of Bedfordshire and Northamptonshire: Vivienne Evans. Anthology of people of yesteryear - arranged alphabetically by village or town.

JOHN BUNYAN: His Life and Times: Vivienne Evans. Highly praised and readable account.

THE RAILWAY AGE IN BEDFORDSHIRE: Fred Cockman. Classic, illustrated account of early railway history.

A LASTING IMPRESSION: Michael Dundrow. A boyhood evacuee recalls his years in the Chiltern village of Totternhoe near Dunstable.

GLEANINGS REVISITED: Nostalgic Thoughts of a Bedfordshire Farmer's Boy: E.W. O'Dell. His own sketches and early photographs adorn this lively account of rural Bedfordshire in days gone by.

BEDFORDSHIRE'S YESTERYEARS Vol 2: The Rural Scene: Brenda Fraser-Newstead. Vivid first-hand accounts of country life two or three generations ago.

BEDFORDSHIRE'S YESTERYEARS Vol 3: Craftsmen and Tradespeople: Brenda Fraser-Newstead. Fascinating recollections over several generations practising many vanishing crafts and trades.

BEDFORDSHIRE'S YESTERYEARS Vol 4: War Times and Civil Matters: Brenda Fraser-Newstead. Two World Wars, plus transport, law and order, etc.

DUNNO'S ORIGINALS: A facsimile of the rare pre-Victorian history of Dunstable and surrounding villages. New preface and glossary by John Buckledee, Editor of The Dunstable Gazette.

PROUD HERITAGE: A Brief History of Dunstable, 1000-2000AD: Vivienne Evans. Century by century account of the town's rich tradition and key events, many of national significance.

DUNSTABLE WITH THE PRIORY: 1100-1550: Vivienne Evans. Dramatic growth of Henry I's important new town around a major crossroads.

DUNSTABLE IN TRANSITION: 1550-1700: Vivienne Evans. Wealth of original material as the town evolves without the Priory.

OLD DUNSTABLE: Bill Twaddle. A new edition of this collection of early photographs.

BOURNE and BRED: A Dunstable Boyhood Between the Wars: Colin Bourne. An elegantly written, well illustrated book capturing the spirit of the town over fifty years ago.

OLD HOUGHTON: Pat Lovering. Pictorial record capturing the changing appearances of Houghton Regis over the past 100 years.

ROYAL HOUGHTON: Pat Lovering. Illustrated history of Houghton Regis from the earliest of times to the present.

GIRLS IN BLUE: Christine Turner. The activities of the famous Luton Girls Choir properly documented over its 41 year period from 1936 to 1977.

THE STOPSLEY BOOK: James Dyer. Definitive, detailed account of this historic area of Luton. 150 rare photographs.

THE STOPSLEY PICTURE BOOK: James Dyer. New material and photographs make an ideal companion to The Stopsley Book.

PUBS and PINTS: The Story of Luton's Public Houses and Breweries: Stuart Smith. The background to beer in the town, plus hundreds of photographs, old and new.

LUTON AT WAR - VOLUME ONE: As compiled by The Luton News in 1947, a well illustrated thematic account.

LUTON AT WAR - VOLUME TWO: Second part of the book compiled by The Luton News.

THE CHANGING FACE OF LUTON: An Illustrated History: Stephen Bunker, Robin Holgate and Marian Nichols. Luton's development from earliest times to the present busy industrial town. Illustrated in colour and mono.

WHERE THEY BURNT THE TOWN HALL DOWN: Luton, The First World War and the Peace Day Riots, July 1919: Dave Craddock. Detailed analysis of a notorious incident.

THE MEN WHO WORE STRAW HELMETS: Policing Luton, 1840-1974: Tom Madigan. Fine chronicled history, many rare photographs; author~served in Luton Police for fifty years.

BETWEEN THE HILLS: The Story of Lilley, a Chiltern Village: Roy Pinnock. A priceless piece of our heritage - the rural beauty remains but the customs and way of life described here have largely disappeared.

KENILWORTH SUNSET: A Luton Town Supporter's Journal: Tim Kingston. Frank and funny account of football's ups and downs.

A HATTER GOES MAD!: Kristina Howells. Luton Town footballers, officials and supporters talk to a female fan.

LEGACIES: Tales and Legends of Luton and the North Chilterns: Vic Lea. Mysteries and stories based on fact, including Luton Town Football Club. Many photographs.

THREADS OF TIME: Shela Porter. The life of a remarkable mother and businesswoman, spanning the entire century and based in Hitchin and (mainly)Bedford.

STICKS AND STONES: The Life and Times of a Journeyman Printer in Hertford, Dunstable, Cheltenham and Wolverton: Harry Edwards.

LEAFING THROUGH LITERATURE: Writers' Lives in Herts and Beds: David Carroll. Illustrated short biographies of many famous authors and their connections with these counties.

A PILGRIMAGE IN HERTFORDSHIRE: H.M. Alderman. Classic, between-the-wars tour round the county, embellished with line drawings.

THE VALE OF THE NIGHTINGALE: Molly Andrews. Several generations of a family, lived against a Harpenden backdrop.

SUGAR MICE AND STICKLEBACKS: Childhood Memories of a Hertfordshire Lad: Harry Edwards. Vivid evocation of gentle pre-war in an archetypal village, Hertingfordbury.

SWANS IN MY KITCHEN: Lis Dorer. Story of a Swan Sanctuary near Hemel Hempstead.

THE HILL OF THE MARTYR: An Architectural History of St.Albans Abbey: Eileen Roberts. Scholarly and readable chronological narrative history of Hertfordshire and Bedfordshire's famous cathedral. Fully illustrated with photographs and plans.

THE TALL HITCHIN INSPECTOR'S CASEBOOK: A Victorian Crime Novel Based on Fact: Edgar Newman. Worthies of the time encounter more archetypal villains.

SPECIALLY FOR CHILDREN

VILLA BELOW THE KNOLLS: A Story of Roman Britain: Michael Dundrow. An exciting adventure for young John in Totternhoe and Dunstable two thousand years ago.

THE RAVENS: One Boy Against the Might of Rome: James Dyer. On the Barton Hills and in the south-east of England as the men of the great fort of Ravensburgh (near Hexton) confront the invaders.

THE BOOK CASTLE, 12 Church Street, Dunstable,
Bedfordshire LU5 4RU
Tel: (01582) 605670 Fax (01582) 662431
Email: bc@book-castle.co.uk

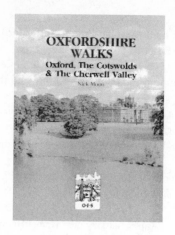
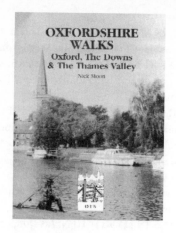

OXFORDSHIRE WALKS VOLUME 1
Oxford, The Cotswolds & The Cherwell Valley

&

OXFORDSHIRE WALKS VOLUME 2
Oxford,The Downs & The Thames Valley

by Nick Moon

Two titles each containing thirty circular walks. The two titles together provide a comprehensive coverage of walks throughout the whole of Oxfordshire (except the Chiltern part already covered in "Chiltern Walks: Oxfordshire and West Buckinghamshire" by the same author). The walks vary in length from 3.3 to 12.0 miles, but the majority are in, or have options in, the 5 to 7 miles range, popular for half- day walks, although suggestions of possible combinations of walks are given for those preferring a full day's walk. Each walk gives details of nearby places of interest and is accompanied by a specially drawn map of the route, which also indicates local pubs and a skeleton road network.

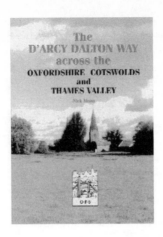

THE D'ARCY DALTON WAY
Across the Oxfordshire Cotswolds
and Thames Valley

by Nick Moon

TITLE: This guide to the D'Arcy Dalton Way; replacing the original guide written and published by the late Rowland Pomfret on behalf of the Oxford Fieldpaths Society in 1987 and now out of print, describes both the route of the D'Arcy Dalton Way itself and eight circular walks using parts of its route ranging in length from 4.0 to 13.4 miles. The text of the guide to the way and each circular walk gives details of nearby places of interest and is accompanied by specially drawn maps of the route which also indicate local pubs and a skeleton road network.

Oxfordshire County Council has kindly organised the acquisition and erection of special signposts for the D'Arcy Dalton Way.

FAMILY WALKS
Chilterns - South

by Nick Moon

This book is one of a series of two, which provide a comprehensive coverage of walks throughout the whole of the Chiltern area. The walks included vary in length from 1.7 to 5.5 miles, but are mainly in the 3 to 5 mile range, which is ideal for families with children, less experienced walkers or short winter afternoons. Each walk text gives details of nearby places of interest and is accompanied by a specially drawn map of the route, which also indicates local pubs and a skeleton road network. The author, Nick Moon, has lived in or regularly visited the Chilterns all his life and has for 25 years, been an active member of the Chiltern Society's Rights of Way Group, which seeks to protect and improve the area's footpath and bridleway network.

The
Book
Castle

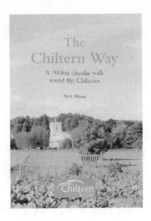

THE CHILTERN WAY

A Guide to this new 133-mile circular Long Distance Path through
Bedfordshire, Buckinghamshire, Hertfordshire & Oxfordshire

by Nick Moon

The Chiltern Way has been established by the Chiltern Society to mark
the Millennium by providing walkers in the twenty-first century with
a new way of exploring the diverse, beautiful countryside which all
four Chiltern counties have to offer. Based on the idea of the late
Jimmy Parsons' Chiltern Hundred but expanded to cover the whole
Chilterns, the route has been designed by the author and is being
signposted, waymarked and improved by the Society's Rights of Way
Group in preparation for the Way's formal launch in October 2000. In
addition to a description of the route and points of interest along
the way, this guide includes 29 specially drawn maps of the route
indicating local pubs, car parks, railway stations and a skeleton road
network and details are provided of the Ordnance Survey and Chiltern
Society maps covering the route.

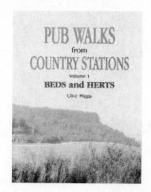
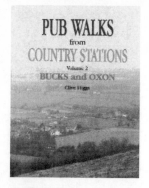

PUB WALKS FROM COUNTRY STATIONS:
Volume 1 - Beds and Herts

&

PUB WALKS FROM COUNTRY STATIONS:
Volume 2 - Bucks and Oxon

by Clive Higgs

Two titles both containing fourteen circular country rambles, each starting and finishing at a railway station and incorporating a pub-stop at a mid-way point.

Volume 1 has 5 walks in Bedfordshire starting from Sandy, Biggleswade, Harlington, Flitwick and Linslade. Together with 9 walks in Hertfordshire starting from Watford, Kings Langley, Boxmoor, Berkhamsted, Tring, Stanstead St.Margaret's, Watton-at Stone, Bricket Wood and Harpenden.

Volume 2 has 9 walks in Buckingham starting from Gerrards Cross, Beaconsfield, Saunderton, Princes Risborough, Amersham, Chesham, Great Missenden, Stoke Manderville and Wendover. Together with 5 walks in Oxfordshire starting from Goring-on-Thames, Cholsey, Lower Shiplake, Islip and Hanborough Station.

The shortest walk is a distance of 4miles and the longest 7 and a half miles.